Anonymous

Centennial of the Methodist Book Concern and dedication of the new Publishing and Mission Building of the Methodist Episcopal Church

Anonymous

Centennial of the Methodist Book Concern and dedication of the new Publishing and Mission Building of the Methodist Episcopal Church

ISBN/EAN: 9783337260033

Printed in Europe, USA, Canada, Australia, Japan

Cover: Foto ©Lupo / pixelio.de

More available books at **www.hansebooks.com**

CENTENNIAL OF THE

METHODIST BOOK CONCERN

AND

DEDICATION OF THE NEW

PUBLISHING AND MISSION BUILDING

OF THE

METHODIST EPISCOPAL CHURCH

———••◆•◆••———

NEW YORK:
HUNT & EATON
150 FIFTH AVENUE
1890

PREFATORY NOTE.

THE Centennial of the Methodist Book Concern having been celebrated with appropriate exercises in connection with the formal opening of the new Publishing and Mission Building, February 11 and 13, 1890, it seems desirable to put in permanent form a brief historical record of the various steps taken in the new building enterprise, together with the addresses made at the Dedication Services and at the Mass-meeting following those services. We therefore issue this little volume to be placed in the archives of the Book Concern and Missionary Society of the Methodist Episcopal Church, and presented to Methodist Historical Societies and Educational Institutions.

HUNT & EATON.

NEW YORK, *Feb.* 20, 1890.

CENTENNIAL

OF THE

METHODIST BOOK CONCERN.

AND

DEDICATION

OF THE

NEW PUBLISHING AND MISSION BUILDING.

------------ ✳✳✳ ------------

Brief History of the New Building Enterprise.

AT a meeting of the Book Committee held in February, 1887, the Book Agents at New York asked authority to sell the two properties then owned and to purchase a site and erect thereon an edifice adapted to the demands of a Publishing House and the wants of the Missionary Society. The Book Committee unanimously approved the proposition, as did also the Board of Managers of the Missionary Society shortly thereafter. A Commission was appointed to carry out the measures proposed, consisting of W. H. Olin, D.D., of the Wyoming Conference; Homer Eaton, D.D., of the Troy Conference; T. N. Boyle, D.D., of the Pittsburg Conference; C. J. Clark, D.D., of the Maine Conference; Clem Studebaker, of Indiana, and the Book Agents and Local Committee at New York. Subsequently G. S. Chadbourne, D.D., of the New England Conference, L. C. Queal, D.D., of the Central New York Conference, and Hon. P. C. Lounsbury, of New York, were appointed in place of Drs. Olin, Clark, and Boyle, who had retired from the Book

Committee. A Building Committee was also appointed, consisting of the Book Agents and Local Committee, representing the Book Concern at New York, and J. M. Reid, D.D., M. D'C. Crawford, D.D., and J. S. McLean, Esq., of New York, representing the Missionary Society. Mr. J. M. Phillips was made Chairman, and Dr. Reid Secretary, of the Building Committee. After the death of Mr. Phillips, Dr. Homer Eaton, who had been elected Book Agent, became *ex officio* a member and Mr. William Hoyt was appointed Chairman of the Building Committee.

The new site on Fifth Avenue was purchased Oct. 31, 1887, and during the General Conference in 1888, on May 23, the corner-stone of the new structure was laid by Bishop Bowman, the senior Bishop of the Methodist Episcopal Church. A very large audience was present, including the Bishops, the members of the General Conference, the Mayor of the city of New York, and many other distinguished persons. Mr. J. M. Phillips, Chairman of the Building Committee, presided, and addresses were made by Colonel E. F. Ritter, of Indianapolis, Bishop Foss, and General Clinton B. Fisk. A brief historic record of the Book Concern, including a catalogue of its publications, was deposited in the corner-stone.

Later the lot on Twentieth Street, adjacent to the new structure, then in process of erection, was purchased for the use of the Book Concern, and the building thereon will be retained, the two upper stories to be used by the engraving department and the two lower stories as a residence for the engineer.

The new edifice, though not fully completed at the time, was occupied Nov. 1, 1889, by the various departments connected with the Book Concern and Missionary Society, except the manufacturing and printing departments, which were removed thither in January, 1890.

The main building is 104 feet 3½ inches on Fifth Avenue and 170 feet on Twentieth Street, and, including the basement, is 130 feet high, embracing, with the basement, nine stories. The first three are of granite, the fourth, fifth, sixth, and seventh are of Baltimore brick, and the eighth and ninth are of granite and brick. The whole structure is built of the best material throughout and is fire-proof.

The Missionary Society owns one third of this new property, and has been able to pay for it without using any of the contributions made to the Society for its general and current work. The sale of the old property at 805 Broadway and 200 Mulberry Street enabled the Agents to complete their two thirds of the new building without leaving any debt upon it.

THE DEDICATION OF THE PUBLISHING AND MISSION BUILDING.

FEBRUARY 11, 1890.

ALL day all through the building workmen and employés were busy putting things to rights and giving the last touches here and there. The preparation ended only after the spacious chapel began to fill for the services at 7:30 P. M. It is a charming room, two stories in height, with a gallery across the end; tastefully carpeted, seated with upholstered opera-chairs. The softly-tinted walls were decorated with fine portraits of Wesley, Asbury, Hedding, Ezekiel Cooper, Durbin, Curry, Wiley, and nearly a score more of the heroic dead. The gallery-front was festooned with the national colors, and a splendid flag, which the day after floated above the building, a present from Mrs. Kate Van Dusen, graced the wall behind the platform.

William Hoyt, Esq., chairman of the Building Committee, was introduced by General Fisk as president of the evening. After singing, "Hasten, Lord, the glorious time," Professor W. F. Whitlock, D.D., chairman of the Western Section of the Book Committee, addressed the throne of grace.

Prayer by Rev. Dr. Whitlock.

O Father, amid all the many gracious blessings that thou hast bestowed upon us we come to-night especially to thank thee for thy Church—the Church that thou didst give the world in the morning of time, in the infancy of the race; that thou hast preserved through the days of Abraham and Isaac and Jacob and David and Daniel, through all the generations and centuries that have come and gone, unto our day. We bless thee, our heavenly Father, for all the institutions that have grown up within thy Church and have served to elevate our race and to bring glory and honor to thy great name. And we come in this evening hour especially to thank thee for the interest represented in this great structure and upon this occasion. We thank thee that many long years ago thou didst put it into the thought and purpose of the fathers to found this organization ; and we bless thee that they sought not only the salvation of the people whom they immediately served, but the salvation of all men ; and we bless thee that they sought not only the conversion of the world, but the instruction of the mind, knowing that all its powers might be employed in the great work that thou hast raised up to thy Church. And we bless thee for that faith and that persistence manifested by the fathers in the standing to this age of these institutions, and in the meeting all these discouragements and disasters. We bless thee for the great growth of these organizations, for the great service they have rendered the Church ; we bless thee that in these organizations very much of the best thought and feeling, of the most positive and strong convictions, have been voiced and have gone out into the households and hearts of thy people. And we bless thee that, when thy Church at home has been made acquainted with the conditions of the nations that have been sitting in darkness, they have undertaken the great business of evangelizing these nations.

We bless thee that thou hast heard the prayers of thy people and brought prosperity and great power to these organizations. We thank thee, Father, for the work that they are now accomplishing ; that in this center of thought and Christian activity there are going out influences and agencies that are blessing millions of homes. We thank thee that they are blessing not only the Church at home, but the Church abroad. We thank thee that here thy Church finds defense and instruction and encouragement. We thank thee that here is interpreted thy word, and that these interpretations are carried to very many of those who are teaching and studying thy truth. For all these things we praise thy name.

We bless thee, our heavenly Father, that thou didst put it into the hearts of those in more immediate authority to select this site and to build this structure; that thou hast been, as we believe, at the head of this enterprise from its beginning until this evening hour; that thou wast here when the foundation-stones were laid; and that thou art here when the cap-stone is brought to its place with rejoicing. Now, bless this organization, these great influences. Bless those who are now in charge; may thy special blessing be with these Agents, these Secretaries, these Boards of Control, these Committees, so that in the great purposes they may undertake there may be found the progressive thought and all the persistence that shall lead thy Church out into still greater enterprises and make it a great instrumentality in thy hands to lead the nations from darkness into light; and, O Lord, we earnestly beseech that from this place evermore in the future there may go out that pure and inspiring and spiritualized thought that shall serve to instruct and build up thy Church every-where. Bless the Church here represented in all its great enterprises and all its interests.

We thank thee for the prosperity in the years that are gone, for its present success and power in the earth, and we pray that its power may be increasingly prospered by thee, and that in the immediate future we may realize that thou art coming in wondrous power into the Church and blessing it in all its agencies. Bring us into the closest and liveliest sympathy with thy will; and may we individually so live that when we come to the hour of death we may then know because thy grace has been imparted to us, because we have been privileged to be led by thy Spirit, that therefore we have no foe, but have fought a good fight and have laid up treasure in heaven ; and unto thee we give all the praise, world without end. Amen.

Homer Eaton, D.D., led in the responsive reading of the 122d Psalm. Following this General Fisk made a brief verbal report for the Building Committee. The grounds cost $450,000, the building $550,000, and the total amount is provided for. In excavating for the foundation the bed of an old river was struck, entailing an extra cost of $17,000 to go down to bed-rock. He referred feelingly to the committee that bought on Broadway and Eleventh Street twenty years ago, only two of whom—Judge Fancher and George I. Seney—are now living, and to John M. Phillips, who was until his death chairman of this committee.

Bishop E. G. Andrews, LL.D., was the first speaker on the programme for the evening.

Address by Bishop Andrews.

Mr. Chairman, I am sure that the Church will receive from the Building Committee this structure with profound satisfaction and great thankfulness. We are reminded of that great architect who was buried beneath the pavement of the magnificent temple which he had erected, and over whose grave were put the words, " If you seek his monument, look around." So think we, sir, of this Building Committee and of their great work. You will pardon me though I say this in your presence, and in the presence of these other brethren who with you have for these two years past wrought so faithfully to the end now reached. Neither you nor they have given to the Church this service in order to secure its grateful recognition. But we who have been witnesses of the constant and anxious labors you have undergone, of the burden thus assumed and patiently borne by men already overburdened, must be permitted to acknowledge with sincere and profound thankfulness the debt which the Church owes to you for the work thus achieved. We rejoice in the unbroken harmony which has ruled, as we are informed, in your councils; and we congratulate you that now at length the Building Committee, having nobly accomplished its aim, may be dissolved.

Sir, we are all gratified with the result. We find no room for criticism. We take note of the convenient and conspicuous location of this edifice; of its massiveness, stateliness, and the chastened beauty of its exterior; of its interior, so spacious, cheerful, convenient, and perfectly supplied with all modern appliances for comfort and the easy transaction of business; of this central hall, the Board-room, so admirably proportioned, so finely finished, so well adapted to the great missionary and ecclesiastical uses for which it is set apart; and of the fact that, large as are our present publishing and missionary transactions, there is ample provision for their future growth in the rooms of the building now leased for other purposes. And with great satisfaction also do we learn from the report of the Building Committee that the great cost of this noble edifice is provided for by the sale of the properties on Broadway and Mulberry Street, and by other funds already accumulated.

This evening, sir, the whole Church, which is here represented, accepts from the Book Committee and from the Missionary Board, through the Building Committee appointed by them, this fruit of a hundred years of our church life, and consecrates it to the Lord of the Church for yet larger and nobler results. With thanks to all who have wrought in this present enterprise, with grateful remembrance of the honored and beloved men who in past years wrought well upon the foundations and walls of our large publishing and missionary organizations, but who have now gone to "the majority," above all, with gratitude to Almighty God, who has so signally prospered the designs of his people, and with high purpose of a better and more effective service, the Methodist Church now enters fully upon the use of this noble structure.

Would that there were associated with us on this happy evening some whom the occasion naturally calls to our remembrance! Perhaps the wish is unnecessary. Perhaps, sir, in the mansions where they now dwell they share our joy and also remember with thankfulness the part they were permitted to take in the long preparation for this hour. Two of them, the calm and judicious Phillips, and the princely J. B. Cornell, both members of the Building Committee, but falling before its work was complete, have already been named. And we tenderly recall others connected with the purchase of the Broadway property, as Durbin, McClintock, Harris, Carlton, Curry, Oliver Hoyt, and W. W. Cornell. And yet others of that and of an earlier generation rise before us whose life-history was intimately connected with the beginning of our publishing and missionary work; but time does not permit special reference to them. Their record is on high.

Naturally to-night we take happy notice of the fact that great progress has been made during the century which now closes in the history of the Book Concern and during the seventy years of our Missionary Society organization.

The enterprise of establishing a publishing house required in the then weak and struggling Methodist Church no ordinary faith and courage. No wonder that they called it a *Book Concern*. Possibly some have not seen the appropriateness of this title. But, sir, you are a business man, and I beg to submit this proposition to you: Given a new and wholly untried business, given a total borrowed capital of $600, given the expenditure of the entire capital upon the printing and binding of books by sundry job-offices in Philadelphia ; given the distribution, on credit, of all these books in the saddle-bags of itinerants from Massachusetts to Georgia; given a new enterprise thus conditioned, and could any one devise a better name for it than Book *Concern?* They must have been under great concern of mind in those days, and especially when, after ten years, John Dickins certified that the indebtedness had risen to $4,500, the assets being still altogether in the good faith and ability of the two hundred or more scantily-paid traveling preachers. *Book Concern*, indeed! We do not have that sort of Concern to-day. Trusting to the combined wisdom of Book Agents, of local committees, of the Book Committee and of the Missionary Board, all entering on the use and sustentation of this structure, with large accumulated capital and unquestioned credit, we are under no apprehension of financial embarrassment. John Dickins occupied with his little Book Concern four different homes during the ten years of its stay in Philadelphia. The Concern has now occupied ten places of business in New York. But even as our itinerancy is getting a little extended, so it may be hoped that this new structure altogether suitable in dimensions, in solidity, in nobility of character, and in adaptation to the work for which it is designed, will be the home of our publising and missionary enterprises for at least a hundred years to come.

No, sir, we have no concern about the stability of this Book Concern. But there are some things about which we are concerned. Not about dividends to Conference claimants, sir, for we doubt whether in the long run it will be found that these are a reliable substitute for, or even an aid to, due appeal to the consciences and hearts of our people in behalf of superannuate and needy preachers. We much prefer that the results of our

great publishing work shall be turned back again into the chan-
nels from which they came, and thus produce larger and better
results. We are concerned that the profits of this great establishment shall provide Methodism with a literature the very best
that Methodism with money can furnish. We are concerned
that our Sunday-school literature shall be, not feebly-good, but
strong, surpassing any thing of the kind which the world now
knows—instructive, attractive, inspiring, and ennobling to our
youth. We are concerned that our periodical literature shall
be delivered from the localisms and personalisms and general
narrowness which, out of the conditions and relations of our
church papers have heretofore seemed almost inevitable. These
are some of our concerns. May we not hope that these also,
like the former financial concern, may soon be allayed? And
then if we can drop, even now as we enter this new edifice, the
old and unattractive title, and substitute for it the simple title
Book House, or, if any prefer, *Publishing House*, this also
would not a little increase with some of us the pleasure with
which we hail this hour.

I have spoken only of the Book House ; let me now recall the
fact that our Missionary Society began its work in like narrow
quarters. Dr. Reid, in his admirable history of our Society,
gives all the statements needed on this point ; tells of the little
band of heroic and hopeful men who formed the Missionary
Society in 1819, tells of the opposition which they encountered
within the Church and of the discouragement of some who
withdrew, one after another, from the management ; tells us also
how with a sublime faith such an one as Joshua Soule said with
prophetic insight : "The time will come when every man who
assisted in the organization of this Society, and persevered in
the undertaking, will consider it one of the most honorable
periods of his life." So said a wise man, and his prophetic

words have been fulfilled. We rejoice this evening as we gather here that from the first annual collections of the Society, amounting in all to $823 04, the Church has so nearly reached the $1,200,000 which the General Committee was able last fall to distribute. So thank we God and take courage.

The past has been spoken of. This building is a record, but it is also a prophecy. Its immovable foundations, its massive walls have in them, we firmly trust, the symbolism of a Church destined to endure through tempest and change to bless far distant generations. Its ample spaces, much of them now occupied under lease by other parties for other business, await resumption for our own purposes, as the enlarging Church shall require. There is here no contentment with past achievements. Such contentment would be the precursor of retreat and decay. On the contrary, this structure foretells not only a stable Church, but a Church which, rising more and more to a comprehension of the times and of God's great purpose in them, shall meet with an increasing intelligence and with fuller missionary consecration the call of a needy world.

There will gather here many years hence, as we devoutly pray, Christian men and women, our successors in Methodism, who will be able to rejoice over a Christian literature, furnished here in part, so pure, so virile, so attractive, so broad, that it shall have in some large degree abated and destroyed the doubtful and pernicious literature that in books and periodicals now floods the land; and they will also, we firmly trust, in that day rejoice over missionary operations and successes compared to which all that we now share in will seem scanty and insignificant.

This building, so please it God, will be the scene of Christian labor and the center of Christian influences that shall not simply touch the margin of distant heathen lands, but penetrate them throughout with the transforming and saving power of the Gospel.

May we and our successors have the wisdom, courage, and faith requisite for such high results.

Address by Earl Cranston, D.D.

Three curiously-related facts may be predicated of this service: It is without precedent in Methodism, yet its preliminaries were arranged more than one hundred years ago, and it is distinctively Wesleyan in type. If our great Jove, from whose brain sprang this modern Minerva—the patroness of learning and armor-bearer to the heroes of our later Iliad— could by any earthly conclave be enticed from celestial delights, surely near this spot would rise his new Olympus.

And who would tremble when he thundered? First, those nearest the summit. Would not the man who made bishops for American Methodism commune with these successors of Coke and Asbury? And should he find one, who had ever knowingly laid hands on a young minister, who had scorned to sell books and *Advocates* would there not be a sound terrible indeed to that un-Wesleyan Bishop, but very comforting to the poor editors and agents by him compelled aforetime to crowd a half hour's eloquence into a seven minutes' speech? And from this solemn moment would not that Bishop—and all the Bishops—vie with the publishers in echoing the original Jovian proclamation, "Be diligent in selling the books," "Spread the magazine; it will do good!"

Such rumblings as might reach our bold Boston seer—who, rivaling the Thunderer himself, laughs at years and antedates his eternal youth by undertaking eleven octavo volumes at three-score and ten—would doubtless be serenely toned. That inter-conference recreation would remind Mr. Wesley of himself and

2

elicit his instant approval, re-enforced by the admonitions, "Foster the literature," "Spread the books!"

How that first American Conference must have touched the old leader's heart by its loyalty to his methods! From that early beginning our Methodism directly and distinctly declared, defined, and defended itself through its own organic press, the fathers esteeming its doctrines, experiences, and polity too precious to be intrusted to any medium not its own; and this hour finds no proposition from any source to abandon or modify the system which has been the guarantee of our doctrinal integrity and is the only sufficient explanation of our matchless connectionalism.

They who have the chief responsibility for its welfare are sometimes alarmed by aggressive individual and local enterprises, just as our devoted secretaries are concerned when unaffiliated movements threaten their respective treasuries—and an officer who is not watchful of his trust is not to be trusted as an officer; yet, if John Wesley were to inspect his parish at this moment, he would doubtless find the Book Concern held in greater esteem than ever before by our people, and discover in the heart of our ministry, as a body, the conviction, positive and unalterable, that no one man, however true, can better adjust the service of the press to the needs of the Church than the Church herself, through her General Conference. Then he would wonder, with us, how a Methodist preacher, having submitted to the Church the most vital and sacred questions growing out of his own call to the holy ministry, could ever assume to decide for the Church matters by her committed only to her highest council.

He would declare, and we would agree, that while one of our number may advocate new projects he cannot consistently project new *Advocates.* He would declare, and we agree,

that as no man amongst us can upon his vows justify
another in using a Methodist pulpit to discredit a cardinal
point in Methodist doctrine, so upon his vows no man
amongst us can justify another in using Methodist patronage
to discredit a cardinal point in Methodist polity; that our
organic press is a cardinal point in our polity, original and
essential; and that on this spot and in this hour, especially,
it were more than undutiful to justify any selfish or ambitious
invasion of the publishing functions of the Church.

But Mr. Wesley was compelled to recognize a law of emer-
gencies, and so must we. Some ministers have projected new
Advocates, and other periodicals, in the spirit of intensest
loyalty. In several centers of population and influence on our
western frontier there are journals edited by presiding elders
or pastors who, without salary, add this labor to their regular
duties. This is no sign of revolution or revolt against the
official press. Commanding influences crystallize so rapidly
under the conditions prevailing in these new centers that prompt
and concerted action in the development of church interests
becomes imperative. Every lifting and propelling force must
be seized upon and our people move promptly to meet opportunities that come once, but never again. In this state of things
a local paper appears to enterprising workers an indispensable
adjunct; but through every venture runs a hope, as loyal to the
Church, as to the new metropolis, that ultimately the sprightly
print may become a great connectional paper. Even these un-
dertakings, however, are not without their perils, and it is well
that they seldom survive the official tenure of their founders,
lest local interests should presently gain permanent ascendency
over our connectional movements, and the latter thus lose the
compactness and momentum which alone have made them
resistless.

Our great founder would doubtless frankly speak upon another question which is now under discussion in some quarters. If the fathers were right in the policy of placing a profit upon their publications when the "societies" as well as the preachers were poor, they would not call upon us to change that policy now that the Church is comparatively rich and the preachers still poor.

There is an unsympathetic if not an unregenerate cadence in the cry for a literature at cost. The minister who by patrimony or matrimony is delivered from fear of want should never echo it. The people who have not paid cost for the Gospel preached to them—much less a profit to the itinerant, on his investment of brain, and heart, and education, and life, and home, and family comforts—will not grudge for his benefit in after years the profit they allow to an ordinary vender of books and periodicals.

I admit that their direct obligation to care for their aged and infirm ministers is not to be thus fully discharged, and that profit is not the sole object of the Book Concern. But the people have never by direct means respectably maintained their disabled pastors in retirement; and the "produce of the Book Concern," while not the single object, was yet of sufficient moment in the plans of its founders to receive constitutional protection. And at this point it is pertinent to inquire, What right have the executors of a trust to consider for an instant any proposition that implies even remotely the practical alienation of property interests committed to their management? For a hundred years the preachers and people of our connection have paid out of their poverty reasonable profits on purchases from the Concern, adding steadily to the capital until now it aggregates more than two and three-quarter millions of dollars, all accumulated under the sacred guarantee above referred to : that their deposits should inure to the benefit of needy ministers, their widows and orphans. Let this trust be justly administered. And while we all agree that our literature may well be offered at prices lower than the average charged by secular houses for similar grades, let no one demand in the interest of this well-to-do generation such concessions from the Book Concern as will leave its lawful beneficiaries without at least a modest interest on their capital. We have paid no large dividends as yet--not even four per cent.—and there is a fearful amount of back interest from the Concern, as well as back pay from the Church, due to these worthy claimants. Encouraged by the abounding prosperity vouchsafed to the business, from the year of her return to the only lawful use of the " produce of the Concern " until this hour, may the Church put far away the day when the civil courts shall be more attentive to the prayer of the humblest claimant on this sacred fund than she herself.

Still communing with the founders of our institutions, let us dutifully accept another word of warning. It is more than a coincidence that, as the links which bind us to our heroic ancestry are broken one by one, the social and religious ties that bind us together are also yielding. The class-meeting was the unit of organization and the school of sympathetic fellowship. It is going from us as the shades of the fathers dissolve into the forgotten past ; and presently the sons who forget the fathers will in like manner be forgotten. Ominous indeed are the facts already confronting us touching the pastoral relation. Its once sacred and scriptural character is being sadly marred by the exactions of convenience, taste, and commercialism attending both its initiation and dissolution. Annual Conferences are seriously debating the problem of entertainment at hotels. Their recurring sessions are no longer to mean more prayers in the homes, more life in the Church, more souls at the altars where they gather. Alas! for these indications that preachers and people are willing to break the blessed intimacy that Christ established between them. If ever the ministry needed, for its own welfare, to be lovingly interested in the people, it is now. If ever our people needed to cultivate affectionate recollections of the men who first led them to God, or have at any time ministered to them in holy things, it is now. And here we have an agency admirable and still unimpaired.

Through the beneficent energies of the Book Concern, founded and maintained by their consecrated efforts, Methodist preachers prolong their ministry, and send their benedictions on to the children's children of those they have served.

Our thoughtful people, on the other hand, find in every book and church periodical a fresh medium of gracious currents between their old-time pastors and themselves, as well as opportunity for deferred payments of gratitude or obligation to those faithful ministers whose poverty in retirement is the heritage of that fidelity in service which won men to God.

Would that no middle-man had ever come between the Concern and the people. Unless initiated through the same baptism into a sympathetic mediatorship, he is a non-conductor of such sentiments as should bind this institution to its friends, and we pay him for putting asunder what God and our fathers joined together.

The apostolic leadership of a Wesley, the wholesome guarantees of the Sixth Restrictive Rule, and the unswerving loyalty of three generations of preachers have, under God, brought us to this scene absolutely unique in history. With increasing admiration for the wisdom that founded our Book Concern I am still for the old rule that protected and strengthened it, and for the rights of the fathers in it, and for such an enlargement of faith and activity through these vastly improved facilities as shall cause a shout of exultant hope on both sides of the swelling flood that yet for a little while rolls between our Israel militant and the host triumphant.

Address by M. D'C. Crawford, D.D.

Mr. Chairman, A few evenings ago I sat reading Dr. Hunt's "Centennial of the Book Concern," and fell asleep and had a dream. I was in that room [pointing to the office of the Missionary Secretaries], sitting conversing with Chaplain McCabe. There was a sharp rap at the door, and the chaplain said, "Come in," and in walked a man of small stature, with a broad brimmed hat, a shad-bellied coat, knee-breeches, a very high white choker and a big cane, with which he marked time as he walked in. As soon as the chaplain saw him, he turned to me, and in an undertone said, "That is John Dickins." He arose and put out his hand and took the visitor's hand and said, "How are you, Brother Dickins? I am very glad to see you." And he introduced him to me, and I told him how glad I was to see him; that I had been reading about him and thinking about him. And he said, "Well, I thought I must come and see this new building; it is making a great noise among us up there." And the chaplain said, "What do you think of it?" "What do I think of it? I do not know what to think of it. Never in the loftiest flights of my imagination did I dream that it was possible that the business I founded one hundred years ago should have expanded to any thing like this." *Just then my door-bell rang, and I woke up to find the vision vanished.* I was very sorry, for I wanted to say to John Dickins that, although he lived in a day of small things, what he did had made possible what those who lived after him had done. He built for Ezekiel Cooper, and Ezekiel Cooper for those who came after him, and those again for their successors, and so for one hundred years this institution has been in course of construction. And it is difficult to say who of the builders deserves the most credit or whose work has been of most consequence. There has been rolled up a magnificent inheritance. What Henry George would call the "unearned increment" has come to the Book Agents of this day: Hunt & Eaton and Cranston & Stowe. Other men labored and they have entered into their labors. I do not agree with Mr. George, that we have no right to an unearned increment, and I do not dispute the right of these Agents to enjoy the wonderful opportunity that is open to them, or the privilege of faithfully discharging the wonderful responsibility that comes upon them. I honor the fathers, but the fathers are never honored by doing right over again what they did. If the fathers lived to-day they would not repeat themselves. They worked in their day and did what was appropriate to their circumstances; those who live now, with other surroundings, must do other work.

And now it seems to me that those who have in charge this great trust, I repeat it, have a wonderful opportunity and a weighty responsibility. I must say I quite agree with Bishop Andrews. I think that we need and may have a better literature. Why, here is this magnificent structure, out of debt, with a large working capital, and what a market: a Methodist population of twelve millions of people!

And now, God forbid that I should seem to reflect upon the past at all; I do not, sir. I say, all honor to those who lived and worked in the past; but not a man among them had the opportunity of the men that live and work now. No longer embarrassed with debt; no longer obliged to consider the mere question of money-making—who can predict the possibilities of the situation! And I believe these brethren, sir, are equal to the emergency! My Brother Cranston will forgive me if I differ from him as to the value of "Book Concern Dividends." Conceding fully the claim of the beneficiaries, I doubt the wisdom of meeting it by a tariff on our literature. The more fully these needy veterans are thrown for support on the people whom they have served the more generous will be the responses. In this section of the Church I am sure that during the years in which the Book Concern has done least for the cause in question the largest increase has been made in the "collection for necessitous cases."

But what is the true business of our publishing house? Is it not to make our literature the best possible, and give it to our whole Methodist population at the lowest market rates? Nay, if possible, undersell the market! I would then take the profits of the Book Concern and buy more brains to put in our periodicals and in our books. I would make them better and at the same time cheapen them. I am not criticising the men who make our periodicals. They are doing noble work. But there are not enough of them. It takes several men to make a modern metropolitan religious weekly, or a first-class review, or a popular Sunday-school journal. We need more editorial force. So, too, I think there should be a larger outlay for authorship, in order to increase the list of books which will commend themselves to the literary public and make the imprint of the house a guarantee of excellence.

Never before in the history of the Church has there been a *chance* for a satisfactory retail Methodist book-store in this city. Now we have an elegant room, and I trust it will be fitted up and so conducted as to compare favorably with any book-store in the land. Our people desire it and are entitled to it. It is their duty to come here and buy books. So I preach and so I practice. But why not make the attraction

irresistible; so that customers will flock here because they are
so well served?

Mr. Chairman, this is something more than a commercial
house; it is more than a mission house. Here are represented
many societies of the Church; here are offices of agents and
editors and secretaries. Here the preachers meet, enough of
them to make an Annual Conference, every Monday morning.
They are the picked men of several conferences. There are
here many things which are representative of the Church.
I wish there were more of them. Every Church society in
this section of the country ought to have an office in this building. It ought to be a great denominational rendezvous. I had
the honor of being a member of the Building Committee.
My associates know that I urged, in season and out of season,
the arrangement for a grand historical room. I would take
the "Library," as it is called, and make it the nucleus of a
great Methodist library, into which I would try to bring every
book ever published by a Methodist press, and I would invite
our missionaries from all over the world to send curiosities. I
would invite historical documents and every thing of every kind
relating to Methodism; and O, dear sir—that the other speakers
should have left it to me to say!—look around here; my heart
is touched as I look at these faces, and then when I think of the
many more that ought to be here! I want room to put
one hundred of them—the men who have made Methodism
famous and who have done honor to our name! Then we
might have a reading-room, where every Methodist newspaper
in the world could be found, so that visitors, when they come
to this city, will not feel that they have seen New York until
they have seen this building. Now, I appreciate the reasons
why what I thought desirable could not be granted. Sir, I
make no reflection upon the Building Committee; I presume

they were wise and right. But the Book Committee hear this; and there are men here who will go to the next General Conference : I hope they will carry the request there. This is a fire-proof building, and is the first suitable place we have ever had for denominational archives. Whatever is done here will only be a beginning. I look to the time when there will be a great historical building for Methodism in this city. Now, sir, all these words, and all the words I have ever spoken in public or in private of this Book Concern, are not only loyal words, but they are tenderly loyal words. I have never been out of harmony with it. Indeed, there now crowd to my lips reminiscences that fill me with emotion. The first wages I ever earned I earned in the folding-room of the old Book Concern in Crosby Street. I was eleven years old. I was obliged to leave school to go to work. I remember the feelings with which I went that first day to that old building, and I remember the first pay-day. That princely Christian gentleman, Beverly Waugh—whose portrait hangs here—was senior Book Agent, and he was paymaster. The business was small in those days, and the Agents paid off the hands. I stood in line with other boys, and when my name was called I went up. I signed my name, and he put in my hands a new Mexican silver dollar. I thought it was the brightest I ever saw, and I have no recollection of any amount of money I ever received making me feel so rich as I felt that day. And then, what surprised me, he seemed to know me. I had recently made a profession of religion and joined the Church on probation. He called me by name; he laid his hand on my head; he prayed that the blessing of God might come upon me. I believe it came ; it has never been withdrawn. And now, as I look back through the years, O what a blessed memory that is! It seems as though all the mercies of my life I trace back to it.

During all my public career of nearly fifty years it has been my privilege to mingle with the good men who have been in one way or another connected with the Book Concern and Mission Rooms. And when I consider the influence they have exerted upon me, how much of the joy of my life, how much of what I am has arisen from my association with them, I feel that I have reason to thank and praise God that I ever knew this institution and that I have held friendly relations with it. I say these things from my love of it, and my brethren in the ministry will bear me witness every-where that this has been my tone on all occasions.

And now I do bespeak for this institution, for its publications, for its interests in every way, their sympathy and their prayers, praying with them, that God will make this great institution a blessing to all the world in all the centuries to come ; that this century may be so glorious and so grand, that so much may be done for God and for humanity, that whoever lives to its close may look back and see a work as great as that which we see as we look back upon the past.

Address by George S. Chadbourne, D.D.

Ten minutes is a small space of time in which to make an address on such an occasion as this. I shall, however, as requested, attempt the difficult task, and if I should transgress the prescribed limits I trust the offense will be condoned on the ground of the largeness of my theme and of the force of habit.

We come here to rejoice together over the completion of this magnificent building, and to dedicate it to its intended uses. I confess to a great interest and gratification in this structure, but they do not arise so much from a view of it as a successful business and financial enterprise, though I find much there that ministers to my pleasure. I am glad that I belong to a Church that owns and manages, with such eminent success, the largest denominational publishing and mission house on the continent, if not also in the world. In the past history and in the present enviable condition of this enterprise I see much which gives to me, as a loyal Methodist, sincere and devout gratitude and joy. Still, these are not the things that have foremost place in my thought to-night, or which, in contemplation, afford me the largest satisfaction. This stately pile, with all the appliances for its work with which it is crowded, has a voice for me, and my brief address will endeavor to interpret that voice as it sounds in my ears. It speaks to me of the mission, the function of the true Christian Church, which I conceive to be twofold. It is, first, to evangelize men, to convert them to the Christian faith and doctrine ; and, secondly, to educate, to culture them therein.

It is clear that the Lord Christ intended his Church to be an evangelizing force in the world. His great commission to it, issued just before his ascension to his triumphant glory, clothed it with that perpetual authority and duty : " Go ye into all the world, and preach the Gospel to every creature." Not to limited places and to select circles, but to all the world and to every creature. Teach the Gospel in every place you can reach and to every man who will hear. What is the Church, any part or branch of it, without this evangelizing element? It is a locomotive without steam ; it can make no progress. It is a human body without the power of assimilation ; it can have no growth. The true Church must be on the move ; it must be aggressive ; it must go to men, and it must assimilate them ; it must build them into itself. I am glad to-night that we can make our confident appeal to the history of Methodism in support of its claim that it has this evidence of being a true Christian Church. " The world is my parish," said its founder, and no true son of Wesley has ever been content with any less field than the world.

From its origin Methodism has been going; it has been on the move to find and preach to men. On this continent it started on horseback, and followed men every-where, East, West, North, and South, as they pushed out in search of home and fortune.

It was scarcely more than firmly planted here when, impelled by its native spirit of evangelism, it organized its Missionary Society and began its larger work of covering the globe with its operations. And I think I am not assuming too much when I say that no other branch of the Christian Church is doing so much to-day to evangelize the world ; no other is carrying and preaching the Gospel to so many of the millions of the earth as our own branch of it. And I cannot conceal my pleasure at the fact that this part of our work—the work of the true Christian Church—demands, needs, such facilities for its prosecution as are furnished by this noble building. We have a right to be glad and rejoice as we come here to dedicate it to such an exalted and worthy use. To my own thought it will be here as a great fountain of living, healing waters, fed by the innumerable streams of the beneficence of the Church, and sending forth in time innumerable streams to water and refresh and save the world.

The second function or mission of the Christian Church, as I conceive it, is to educate, to culture men in the Christian faith and doctrine. And here again I do profoundly rejoice that my own Church is second to none. No branch of the Church is doing so much to promote in the world an intelligent, well-grounded, and, therefore, rational religious faith. Methodism has never held to the idea that ignorance is the parent of devotion. On the contrary, it has from its origin utterly repudiated that false and mischievous assumption. Its whole history, from its birth in Oxford down to this hour, is the emphatic denial of that charge or insinuation, sometimes heard, that Methodism was rather in sympathy with an uneducated ministry and an uncultured membership. It has been the glory and boast of Methodism that it has been in hearty sympathy with the people —with all the people. It has proclaimed its mission to be, to preach the Gospel to the poor as well as to all others who would hear it. But it has never counted ignorance, illiteracy, as a virtue, but has done more than any other religious body to do away with them, and to raise up a membership whose piety should rest on knowledge and intelligence. To-day, in this place, amid the surroundings of this hour, I can again make my confident appeal to its history, and rest the case there. Two men were sent from God, and the name of each was John. Each came for a witness, to bear witness to the truth as to the mission of the Church. The first was John Wesley, the well-equipped collegian, the profound scholar, the indefatigable student, the facile, ever busy writer. We have a right to make our boast that Methodism was born in a university—in proud and venerable Oxford—born out of the heaven-illuminated soul and the heaven-baptized heart of one of the intellectually largest men of his own or almost any age. Rarely does England send blazing across the firmament of this world brighter, clearer intellect than that of John Wesley. He has justly been the wonder and the admiration of the foremost men of his own and of later times. We turn to this first John, our founder; and while we find him burning with a quenchless zeal to evangelize men, to lead them into Christian life and experience, scarcely less was his zeal to have them well-informed as to the great essential truths on which that life and experience were founded. Wesley was an immense publishing house in himself, furnishing out of the masterful resources of his own wonderfully-endowed nature, author, editor, publisher, and distributor. His pen, no less than his life, emitted light upon the pathway of all who became his followers. His aim was first to flood the souls of men with the regenerating light of the Holy Spirit, and thus set them in the road heavenward ; and then, that they might walk intelligently, successfully therein, flood that road with the clear electric light of knowledge. And that aim has been steadily kept in view by Methodism ever since; never has it been lost sight of. This it was that brought forth our second John, he whose name was Dickins.

Well may we recall and speak of him here to-day; well may we seek to estimate the debt which Methodism owes to him. Methodism saw its need of books, of a literature with which to culture its followers, to instruct and train them in Christian truth, as interpreted by itself. Whence should they come? Methodism was small and poor; but in this hour of its need came the second John. How has that handful of corn in the top of the mountains—that little six hundred dollars loaned to Methodism by John Dickins—how has it come to shake like Lebanon, and the fruit thereof to fill the earth! Behold these stately buildings, these millions of capital, these crowded rooms and shelves, these ceaselessly active presses pouring out their tons of Christian literature, and sending them on apocalyptic wings over the world! In all this let us behold what God hath wrought. But all this is only familiar history, household words, to world-wide Methodism. Thus, led by the hand of God, Methodism has risen from the small beginnings of John Dickins, and his little room in Philadelphia, up to this grand structure, and these abundant and perfect appointments for this part of its great work. It is surely well for us, in this day of such large things, to remember that of the small things, and to cherish gratefully the memory of the men, sent of God, through whose faith, self-denial, and heroism we have reached this grand estate.

But I must stop, for my time has expired. But the theme is a grateful one, and I have it in my brain and heart to say more. Standing here to-night, after this lapse of a hundred years of Methodism as an educating, culturing force in this land, an illuminator of the pathway of men in Christian truth and life, there comes to me a vision of what may be, of what we may expect will be, at the close of another hundred years. I cannot delay you to portray that vision, nor indeed is it necessary that I should do so. For, if what we now behold and celebrate be the fruitage which a century has brought from so small a planting, what may we believe our children shall behold as they come together to celebrate the second centennial of Methodism as an evangelizing and educating force in the world! If the little one of 1789 has become a thousand in 1889 what will the thousand of 1889 have become in 1989? May those who shall be then alive to behold it be even more loyal and devoted to our Methodism than are we, and may that Methodism then be even more mighty as an agency to win men to God and train them for his service.

At the conclusion of Dr. Chadbourne's address the chairman placed the magnificent property in the hands of Hon. Amos Shinkle, chairman of the Book Committee, and, in the absence of Judge Fancher, of Dr. Sandford Hunt, treasurer of the Missionary Society, who, in turn, presented it to Bishop Andrews for dedication. In doing this Mr. Shinkle said:

BISHOP, On behalf of the Book Committee of the Methodist Episcopal Church, the happy duty devolves upon me to present to you our part of this building to be dedicated to the service of Almighty God, through the publishing interests of the Church, and may God grant that Scriptural holiness may be extended more and more over all lands through the instrumentality of the Book Concern!

3

Dr. Hunt said:

On behalf of the Missionary Society of the Methodist Episcopal Church it gives me great pleasure to present to you that portion of this building owned by the Missionary Society, to be dedicated to the service of God and the spread of Christ's kingdom throughout the earth.

Receiving the building at their hands the Bishop led the congregation in a most comprehensive and devout prayer of dedication. After the doxology the venerable and beloved Dr. William Nast pronounced the benediction and the audience slowly dispersed, with old-time Methodist greetings and admiring loiterings through such portions of the magnificent structure as remained open for inspection.

METROPOLITAN OPERA-HOUSE MEETING.

THE Metropolitan Opera-house was crowded with enthusiastic Methodists on the occasion of the mass meeting, Thursday night, February 13. Bishop Andrews presided. Dr. A. E. P. Albert, of New Orleans, read the Scriptures. Chaplain McCabe, Senior Missionary Secretary, led the singing. Dr. John M. Reid offered the following prayer:

Prayer by J. M. Reid, D.D.

O Lord God of Abraham, of Isaac, and of Israel, God of our fathers, our God, blessed be thy name forever! Both riches and honor come of thee, and thou reignest over all, and in thine hand it is to make great, and to give strength. All things come of thee, and of thine own have we given thee. We, who in time past were not a people, are now the people of God, a chosen generation, a royal priesthood, a peculiar people, that we should show forth the praises of him who called us out of darkness into his marvelous light. Thou hast quickened us together with Christ, hath raised us up together, and made us to sit together in heavenly places in Christ Jesus. O God, we have assembled to-night to be glad in thy name, to render thee thanksgiving and praises for what thou didst for our fathers and for what thou hast done for us. Thou didst give them to see, as with the light of noonday, that it was no part of thy divine purpose that any human being should perish, but rather that all should turn unto thee and live. It was a distinct and burning revelation to them of divine goodness in all its Christly richness, and of saving grace in all its unspeakable freeness and

fullness. Glory be to God! Thou didst give them also tongues
of fire with which to proclaim, the world wide over, " whosoever
will, let him come and partake of the waters of life freely."
O how we thank thee that thou didst reveal to them, through
thy word, that the Spirit of God itself would bear witness to
the believing soul that it was born of God, and that we might
know our sins forgiven and feel the joys of sonship. Yes, ever
blessed God, thou didst put this experience into their hearts,
in fact sent forth the Spirit of thy Son into their hearts, crying,
Abba, Father! They sang it, they shouted it, they preached
it until now millions in all lands are testifying that they are
pardoned and saved, that they have passed from death unto life.

We thank thee, O Father, that thou didst lead us at a very
early day to put this Gospel on fire upon printed pages, and to
send them out as leaves of the tree of life for the healing of the
nations. We thank thee for a hundred years of subsequent
prosperity. We look around our great building and we cry
out with overflowing gratitude, "What hath God wrought!"
Help us, O Lord, to be glad as we ought, and rejoice to-night.
O for a baptism of the old fire, that we may shout aloud thy
praise! So unfold, we entreat thee, the history of thy dealings
with us to the minds of those who are to address us on this occasion that they shall vividly conceive and powerfully express
the truth. Let a mighty volume of song so well up from these
thousands of hearts that, as in the days of old, all can see

> How happy are they,
> Who the Saviour obey,
> And have laid up their treasure above!

Above all we beseech thee, O thou God of our fathers, abide
with us, and let it be forever; continue to impart efficiency and
success to the Church in all its departments. Let this great
press that we are driving by steam become a yet mightier voice

to preach thy word. Keep it on the side of truth, of righteousness, of temperance, of freedom, of holiness. Endow it, in all its departments, with the spirit of holy consecration. From all false doctrines, heresies, and schism, from all contempt of thy word and commandments, from all indorsement of ungodly words or deeds, good Lord, deliver us. Continue to lead on this missionary host into the darkness still overshadowing our world, till there shall be a band for Jesus on every isle that gems the sea and in every land on which the sun shines. Preserve us as a people pure in doctrine, fervent in spirit, burning in zeal, consecrated in property, united in love, truly humble in spirit, and simple-minded, wise in all our methods, adding daily to us such as are saved. Keep us from growing proud as we become great, or from becoming self-important as we become intellectual. Send down upon our Bishops to-night, all of them, wherever they are, a fresh anointing that will inspire them anew to lead the hosts of God's elect. Give to all the pastors of the flock the Spirit of the great Shepherd, that each may take those of his own fold into green pastures and to the living springs.

Come now, O Lord, we beseech thee, into that house that we have builded for thee ! Come thou and the ark of thy strength. Take up thine abode there. Preside over all the great boards that may find a lodgment beneath that roof. Restrain them from all wrong-doing and show them the way to most enlarged and glorious enterprises for thee and for our redeemed race.

All that thou hast given us, that great building, those temples over the land filled with their hundreds of thousands, those institutions of learning where sages sit to train our youth, those millions of dollars that are in our coffers, the honors that garland our brows, are all from thee, but would be nothing without thee. Great God, give us thyself ! May the Shekinah that beams upon our holy places never grow dim, but as the centu-

ries roll round let us become more and more able to glorify thy
name, more and more fully equipped for all the great duties of
the future, and then in thy presence, when earth has passed
away, take our full share in crying, with the triumphant host
before the throne, "Blessing, and glory, and wisdom, and thanksgiving, and honor, and power, and might, be unto our God for
ever and ever." Amen.

The first address was by Bishop Foss, on "Tongue and Type
Joint Agencies in Evangelization." He spoke as follows:

Address by Bishop Cyrus D. Foss, D.D., LL.D.

The tongue and the pen are the two greatest forces in the
world. Thought underlies all action and propagates itself and
multiplies its power by words. Words, spoken or written, have
sharpened all swords, loaded all cannon, kindled the fires of all
revolutions, built and destroyed nations, turned the world on its
hinges. Words, immortal words, forged into the thunderbolt
of our Declaration of Independence, and made good by seven
years' war, broke the galling chains of thirteen feeble colonies
and made them free and independent States. And other words
in that Constitution which Mr. Gladstone declares "the most
wonderful words ever struck off at a given time by the brain
and purpose of man," welded those discordant colonies into a
nation and sounded far out among the nations, and far down
the ages, the glad evangel of "government of the people, by
the people, for the people."

By these stepping-stones let us ascend the highest interests
of mankind. Christianity began its career as a tongue of fire,
but at once linked itself with the pen. On the day of Pente-
cost assembled thousands were startled by the mighty outburst
of its power, and its character as a burning proclamation was
suggested by tongues of flame on the brows of its chosen mes-

sengers; but then their chief spokesman immediately linked this scene with the writings of the prophet Joel. The Saviour himself used both tongue and pen. He did not, indeed, with his own hand write a single word which has come down to us, but he set his seal on the ancient writings by saying: "Search the Scriptures;" and, "If they hear not Moses and the prophets neither will they be persuaded though one rose from the dead." He also guided hands which held pens inspired by himself. St. Luke, in his second treatise, describes his gospel as a record of what Jesus "began to do and teach." It was only the beginning. Several books of the New Testament might be more fitly named. It would teach a deeper truth if the fifth of these books were styled the "Acts of the Lord Jesus Christ by the Apostles;" and the sixth, "The Epistle of the Lord Jesus Christ to the Romans by the Pen of Paul;" and the last," The Revelation of the Lord Jesus Christ to the World Through the Soul of John."

In every great forward movement Christianity has wielded both tongue and pen. Luther used both. Before the Diet of Worms he said: "Here I stand; I can do no other; God help me, Amen." But before that time he had put himself on record by the ninety-four theses which he wrote and nailed to the door of the church at Wittenberg. Afterward, when outlawed and not permitted to speak, and imprisoned in the castle of the Wartburg, he rendered one of his greatest services to the Reformation, with the pen, by translating the Bible into the common language of the German people. He also put his profoundest beliefs into permanent form in commentaries; one of these found out John Wesley in the very crisis of his religious life, and brought him to the joyful knowledge of salvation—thus making Martin Luther the lineal grandfather of Methodism.

Wesley spoke and wrote incessantly. What he did in either of these lines would have been enough for three men of average industry. All the world knows him as the most tireless of itinerant evangelists and is coming to know him as one of the most prolific of authors.

In this respect Methodism has always been animated by the spirit of its founder. It has gone every-where, blowing trumpets and setting types. Primarily it has always been, in every land to which it has gone, a glorious proclamation of gospel grace. It has felt the great commission as a hurricane at its back and a fire in its heart. "Go ye!" has been its watchword. But wherever it has gone, and got a foothold, and stopped long enough to get its breath and look around, it has at once sent for a printing-press. So it is most fit that these missionary secretaries and Book Agents should sit together on the same platform and be housed within the same magnificent walls; nay, that the senior publisher and the missionary treasurer should actually be condensed into one person.

In the monumental edifice which, in the first decade of the second century since its formal organization, the Methodist Episcopal Church has erected, posterity will see, enshrined in massive and graceful architecture, very much of the spirit and purpose of the Methodism of to-day. If there are "sermons in stones and books in running brooks" surely some voices must be pouring forth from that magnificent pile. Shades of Asbury and Dickins and Soule and Bangs and Waugh and Durbin and your co-laborers, ye who with eloquent voice and printed page laid so broadly and grandly the massive foundations on which it is our exalted privilege to build, speak to us from the celestial battlements over which ye look down upon us at this hour! Methinks they answer in adoring wonder, "What hath God wrought!" Let us take up the strain, "What hath God wrought" through these two institutions which they founded and conserved and loved!

Through our beloved Missionary Society "what hath God wrought!" At its first anniversary, just seventy years ago, its aggregate collections for the first year were found to be $823 64; and a speaker who ventured in his impassioned oratory to predict that the time would come when the churches within the limits of the Baltimore Conference alone would raise a like amount in a single year was thought to be a Utopian dreamer. Last year the income of the Society was $1,130,000. In our country this Society (together with its twin sister, the Board of Church Extension,) has done more than any other agency to lay the moral and religious foundations of twenty of our newer States and Territories and to speed the flight of the twin angels of moral and legal temperance, with radiant faces and drawn swords, over the vast prairies of Iowa, Kansas, and the two Dakotas. Into many foreign lands it has also gone, and gone to stay until the rosy light of the millennium shall flood the whole earth. It has gone to them to plant churches and schools and orphanages and hospitals and presses, to use its siege-guns and flying artillery and infantry and cavalry, and every possible new arm of effective service, until the militant Church shall become the Church triumphant. In India and China already three hundred dusky Orientals, led by us into the ministry of the word, are sounding the call of gospel grace through the ranks of the heathenism they have lately abandoned; and twelve thousand more, whose hearts God has "strangely warmed," kneel with our missionaries around the holy sacrament of the Saviour's death. Our latest reports from India bring tidings of pentecostal blessing. At a camp-meeting on the Rohilkund District last December two hundred and thirty persons were forward for prayer in a single day, and nearly all were joyfully converted. Our veteran missionary, the Rev. Dr. E. W. Parker, presiding elder of the district, says: "Our baptisms last year were 1,457, this year 2,966, and if the brethren during 1890 only baptize the present inquirers they will report quite 4,000."

Toward these grand results on both sides the great Pacific—here and yonder—our printing-presses have wrought mightily. Who can tell how much they have had to do at once with the essential spirit of Methodism and with its actual progress, with the training of its workers and the spread of its work? What scales can weigh the sacred aroma of the hymns of Charles Wesley? And what mathematics can estimate the sum total of the healing influence which they have poured forth into the miasma of the world's sin? Well was it for the world that Methodism was born and reared in a renowned university, and that, in the very first generation of its history, it produced such authors as Wesley and Clarke and Watson and Fletcher —men whose amplitude of learning, theological insight and soundness and polemic power have commanded respect wherever the English language is read. So high a Calvinistic theological authority as Dr. James W. Alexander paid the following tribute to Watson: "Turretine is in theology *instar omnium*. Making all due allowance for the difference of age, Watson, the Methodist, is the only systematizer, within my knowledge, who approaches the same eminence; of whom I use Addison's words: 'He reasons like Paley and descants like Hall.'" John Fletcher was the very model of a master in religious controversy. His satire was as keen as his logic, as merciless as his character was saintly. His "Checks" can never become obsolete so long as the errors he combated need to be checked. Evangelical Arminianism, which in our time has so nearly snowed under the old type of Calvinism, owes to these authors and their successors, and to the preaching inspired by their writings, a debt not yet fully acknowledged.

Two incidents may suffice to illustrate this quiet working of

Methodism beyond its own ecclesiastical pale in contributing toward a movement scarcely less than a revolution. When my father was a young circuit preacher on the east end of Long Island he was moved by the criticisms rife in those times to announce one Sunday that the next time he came around the circuit he would read from the Westminster Confession and show how its doctrines differed from those of Methodism. This announcement filled the little church, and brought out especially the Presbyterian elders, one of whom on his way home complained that a Methodist preacher should read any thing publicly from the Westminster Confession, and added, "And then he read the very worst things in it."

Sixty years have passed, and now our Presbyterian friends are struggling in an agony over that Confession to cast out those "very worst things." We most candidly wish them success in so laudable an effort; but some of them are not ready for it yet. President Patton, of Princeton, says: "It must amuse the theologians of the Methodist Church to notice that Presbyterian office-holders are trying to persuade the Church which honors Charles Hodge and Henry B. Smith as its great dogmatic theologians to go over bodily to the platform of the Remonstrants." But the editor of our chief weekly tells us that Henry B. Smith, many years ago, published an article designed to show that "there is no insuperable difficulty in the way of a union of Presbyterians and Methodists." Well, they seem now actually to be coming "to the platform of the Remonstrants." Let them come singing:

> " For the love of God is broader
>   Than the measure of man's mind,
>   And the heart of the Eternal
>   Is most wonderfully kind."

We who have tried no other platform will welcome them,

and " He who tasted death for every man " will bless the banns. Go on, tongue and pen, Missionary Society and Book Concern, in the great work to which your Lord has called you in many lands! Be quick to answer his summons : "Go teach all nations." Hold your place in the front ranks of his ever-advancing host. Cherish the spirit of the world-ranging missionary of early Methodism—Bishop Coke. It is said of him that in his middle life, when once very sick, he had this striking experience : he felt himself borne by an angel out of this life and upward, through surging waves of glory, toward the eternal city. He asked to be borne at once into the presence of John Wesley, but was told his work was not finished, and he could not enter heaven then. Filled with unutterable regret he said : " Must I return ? "   " So God wills," said the angel ; and Coke answered, " If I must go back, let me go and *blaze until I die.*" He at once returned to consciousness, rapidly recovered, and blazed until he died. Until his death he represented in his own person the whole of the missionary operations of Methodism ; he lavished on them a large fortune, gave more money for religious work than any other Methodist, if not any other Protestant of his own time, and at last, on his way to plant missions in the Orient, gave his body to be buried in the Indian Ocean.

God grant that the multiplying myriads of the tongue and types of Methodism may be vitalized with the same evangelizing spirit ; that they may " blaze," not, indeed, until they die, but until, in the holy influence they shall have exerted, they shall live forever amid the splendors of the eternal world !

At the conclusion of Bishop Foss's address Bishop Andrews arose and said :

Very many of our saints of Methodism, who have departed for a little while, always have turned with a loving heart toward the Church again when they have reached the heights of prosperity in their usefulness. One such is here with us to-night, and I am very happy to be able to introduce to you this evening a man very well known in New York, the Rev. Dr. Thomas Armitage, of the Baptist Church.

In his reply Dr. Armitage spoke as follows :

Remarks by the Rev. Dr. Armitage.

I hope to be pardoned for this intrusion. I hold in my hand two or three manuscripts of Methodism. They have been locked up in my desk possibly for a score of years, and I have felt that the occasion to-night would be a fitting one to hand them to the people who should own them. First, there are two manuscripts of as distinguished men as the Methodist Church ever produced either in this or any other country. The first is a sketch, I take it, of a lecture by Dr. Wilbur Fisk on " The Death of Christ." It comes to me directly from his study through the hand of his wife and a mutual friend. It is merely a collection of watchwords evidently intended to guide him in his address, but you get a very comprehensive idea of the whole sweep of his mind on that thought—the death of Christ. It is in his own handwriting. The other is a series of notes upon certain portions of the Epistle of Paul to the Romans, covering eight finely-written pages, in the handwriting of John Summerfield. His biographer says that he was an enthusiast in his study of the Pauline literature as it is contained in that book ; and here we have some of the results of close application. These pages were presented to me by his sister, Mrs. Blackstock, many years ago. She said she would present them to no other person on earth but myself. They were the last manuscripts of the sort that were left in her hands. She had the kindness to say that in many things I reminded her so much of her brother that she believed they would be well taken care of if she left them with me. I said to her,

" Have you any thing else that is particularly from your brother?" She said, " Yes, I have the most precious thing that he left on earth ; namely, an ivory pocket memorandum-tablet which he carried in his pocket for years. I found it in his pocket after his death, and it is covered with memoranda from his own hand : I will give you it if you will faithfully promise me that it shall be kept as a sacred trust." I promised always to care for it, and I have kept my promise, and now after nearly a quarter of a century I think these two productions of these princes of Methodism should belong to the Methodist Episcopal Church, and I would like to present them to Bishop Andrews to-night, desiring that he will put them in a glass case, or in some other convenient and safe repository, to be kept in your beautiful new building with all the other relics of the dead and the productions of the living that there find a home.

Bishop Andrews accepted these valuable gifts with thanks, assuring the generous donor that they should be preserved with greatest care.

Many letters of regret were received. Dr. Howard Crosby's letter was read by General Fisk.

Dr. Sandford Hunt was the next speaker. His subject was " The Book Concern," of which he said :

Address by Dr. Hunt.

We are assembled to-night, according to the programme in your hands, to celebrate the completion of one hundred years in the history of the Methodist Book Concern and the seventieth year in the history of the Missionary Society of the Methodist Episcopal Church. One hundred years in the march of centuries in the history of the world is but a small fraction in the ever-moving procession ; but in the history of individuals or institutions it may bound the time of their origin, record, close, and burial.

Every organization, like every child, must pass through a period of growth to reach the maturity and strength of manhood. One hundred years ago, at the time of the establishment of the Book Concern, the Methodist Episcopal Church was but five years of age, and numbered only fifty-eight thousand members. The United States had but two years before adopted a federal Constitution, and only three and a half short months before the opening of the first book store in Philadelphia, Washington, the first President elected under the Constitution, had been inaugurated in this city of New York.

There was not at that time, nor for twenty-five years thereafter, a religious newspaper in the United States. Of the forty-three papers, political and local, published in 1789, the combined circulation did not equal in amount of matter the New York *Christian Advocate* of to-day. The itinerant ministers, upon whom depended the success of the new enterprise, traveled on horseback, fording rivers long yet to remain innocent of bridges, and penetrating forests which wild beasts had held with undisputed claim.

It was in the midst of such surroundings that the fathers of the Church laid the foundations of our Book Concern, which has attained a magnitude so honorable to the Church to-day. They had no experience to guide them and no models to copy or warn them. They were stimulated, however, by the record of the founder of the Church, who yet lived to give his benedictions to our men and their work. Mr. Wesley had traversed Great Britain and other parts of the world for fifty years, traveling 250,000 miles—ten times the distance around our world—chiefly on horseback. He had preached on the way 42,000 sermons, and yet he found time to write and publish thirty solid volumes and translate and publish one hundred and twenty more.

He required the preachers whom he sent out to severe fields of labor to be students. If they were unwilling or unable to form studious habits Mr. Wesley dismissed them from his ranks. The first preachers of the Methodist Episcopal Church felt the need of books quite as strongly as Mr. Wesley. Some were imported from England. The regular trade would not run the risk of remunerative sales. Hence, five years after the organization of the Methodist Episcopal Church, John Dickins, pastor of a church in New York city, was sent to Philadelphia to found a bookstore and publishing house. With his borrowed capital of $600 he flung his banner to the breeze and began his work. In addition to his agency as Book Steward he was pastor of a church. Debts and embarrassments were inevitable. To crown the burdens, Mr. Dickins died of the yellow fever in 1798, leaving a debt of $4,500, which at that time was a formidable one. When Ezekiel Cooper, his successor, grappled with the difficulties of the situation, he was requested by the Philadelphia Conference, in 1802, to pack up the whole Concern stock —books, accounts, and all—in his trunk, and leave for Baltimore. This he declined to do; but two years afterward he removed the business to New York.

If Philadelphia dismissed the Book Concern without tears of regret we do not learn that any jubilee of welcome greeted its advent in New York. Within twenty years the business was removed from one street to another seven times. In 1833 lots were purchased on Mulberry Street, where our manufacturing has been carried on until last month. In 1836 the whole structure was devoured by fire. By this time the whole Church had felt the importance of her publishing house, and contributions were furnished amounting to $89,994 98, New York city now taking the lead. In that unpretentious building products have been sent out which, in connection with the Western house, amount to $50,000,000, and, what is more remarkable, one half of this amount has been printed and sold within the last sixteen years.

In 1820 a branch house was established in Cincinnati. In twenty years it became a separate corporation, and its history is quite as successful as our own. In the summaries which I present, both of capital and products, I include the business of that house, as the general term, "The Methodist Book Concern," includes both.

That little capital of $600—borrowed one hundred years ago —has now become $2,500,000 ; and while this has been accumulating the Book Concern has paid out, for various purposes outside of its own business, more than the $2,500,000 now retained as working capital. Of this sum over $700,000 has been given for the support of superannuated preachers, widows, and orphans ; and last year, and this, we are giving $100,000, and the shadow of this sum will never be less !

We would naturally expect a rapid increase in business because of the marvelous increase of our membership. In 1790 the number of inhabitants in the United States was about 4,000,000 ; the number of members in the Methodist Episcopal Church was 58,000. The increase in the nation has been fifteen-fold ; the increase in the membership of the different branches of Methodism has been at least sixty-fold, or four times that of the population.

As rapidly as the Church has increased, both actually and relatively, in membership, it has increased in its patronage of the Book Concern more rapidly than in numbers. In 1848 our membership was 644,229. The sales of the Book Concern during the quadrennium closing with 1848 were $612,625 19, or a little less than one dollar a member. During the last quadrennium, closing with 1888, our membership was 2,093,395.

4

The sales of the Book Concern, East and West, during the period were $6,920,743 17—over three dollars a member.

Fifty years ago we had one copy of our church papers for adults for fifteen of our members. If we include semi-official papers, most of which are published under the sanction of Annual Conferences, we now have one for eight.

In our Sunday-school department the increase has been even more remarkable. In 1850 we had 514,429 connected with our Sunday-schools. The entire number of papers published for these schools was 77,363, or about one for every seven scholars. In 1889 we had in round numbers 2,000,000 in our schools; but we published in all over 3,000,000 of papers, or one and a half for each scholar and teacher. The increase in our Sunday-schools was four-fold; the increase in our papers was forty-fold. Our famous statistician, Dr. Dorchester, in his *History of Christianity in the United States*, estimates the entire value of religious literature published in the United States by the different religious denominations up to this time at $144,000,000. Of this the Methodist Episcopal Church has issued $50,000,000, over one third of the whole, and over one half of this amount during the past sixteen years.

And now what is the result? The largest Protestant Church in the United States consolidated into unity! The two great factors which have brought about this unity are the unity of our episcopacy and the centralization of our publishing interests under the direct sanction and control of the Church. We have had no conventions to bring about a revision of our creeds; and yet the Methodist Episcopal Church favors no looseness or uncertainty on questions of Christian doctrine or morals. Every person is publicly asked, before admission to the fellowship of the Church, the same disciplinary questions, chief among which is this: "Do you believe the doctrines of the Holy

Scriptures as set forth in the Articles of Religion of the Methodist Episcopal Church?" Every minister pledges his solemn faith to preach and maintain them. The same books are placed in the Course of Study for every one of the nine hundred ministers who are admitted to the ranks of the itinerancy each year. The Bishops of the Church are a unit in administration, and the little mighty Book of Discipline is their omnipotent guide. One of our Bishops presides in a Conference in Montana to-day, and next week in Georgia, and the next in New England. The next Bishop who presides in the New York Conference lives in Texas. The one who presides in the New York East resides in San Francisco. Our own resident Bishop of New York returned only last week from an episcopal visit to Japan and China, and from the time he left New York until his return he was not necessarily out of the bounds of an Annual Conference or mission of the Methodist Episcopal Church except when he was on the ocean.

It is under such superintendency that the Church has been consolidated and solidified into unity during the one hundred years. The ministry is *one body*, whatever subdivisions may be convenient for Annual Conferences. The centralization of our publishing business is the logical outcome of a connectional Church. The Book Concern is not only a mighty bond of union, but the unity of our ministry renders its maintenance an absolute necessity. At our General Conferences, where the whole Church is assembled through its representatives, men are chosen as editors of books and papers who are believed to be worthy of trust as expounders of our doctrines and polity. The Book Concern sends out to the world products only which these trusted officers provide. The three million Sunday-school helps sent out from New York and Cincinnati, for use in our Sunday-schools every Sunday, have all passed the scrutiny of the editor chosen by the General Conference. They bear his indorsement that they are healthful and saving. The children in the Sunday-school are taught the same doctrines that are enforced in the pulpits. Our young ministers purchase the literature we publish, and they are in fact our only authorized agents for its dissemination.

The Methodist Book Concern is the great center to which the Methodist Episcopal Church looks for its supply of Christian literature, as the pulpit is the center of each congregation for religious instruction. Is it a matter of surprise, then, that there has never been a secession from the Church on doctrinal grounds? In fifty years not fifty ministers have left our pulpits on account of disagreement with the doctrinal standards of our Church, and from present indications the whole Protestant Church will soon officially indorse them.

It is conceded to-day that we have an educated ministry; and yet, as much as we value a classical course, not exceeding twenty per cent. of those who enter our ministry are graduates of college. Every one of these men, however, must graduate in the Conference course of study. Every young man, as he presents himself at the door of the Conference, is handed a schedule of eleven solid volumes for his first year and notified that he must master these books before he can take one step in advance. You may examine the catalogues of our colleges, and you will find that the studies required in the whole course necessary for graduation in any one of them are not as extensive or severe as those in the four years' course required of every Methodist preacher. Whether these courses have for their chief end the attainment of knowledge or mental discipline, ours will not suffer by the comparison. The Methodist Book Concern is the magazine from which they draw their supplies. It is the educator of our ministry as well as its agent. Thus it has been for a hundred years, and thus it must be for a hundred years to come.

As the financial outcome of the century the Agents and the Book Committee, under whose supervision they act, had the high honor on Tuesday evening last of presenting to the Church the grand fire-proof structure on Fifth Avenue, with its presses driven with steam and its apartments illuminated with lightning, and all free from debt!

With such a consummation for this century what prophet will arise to tell us what shall crown the work of the new century upon which we have entered? Standing upon our mount of vision and gazing over the past we say, All honor to the noble men who laid the foundation, deep and strong, upon which we have been able to build such a structure! Their record is the broad Church which now covers every nation on earth.

The long, weary road of the itinerant, whose saddle-bags were our bookstores, whose sermons aroused into holy enthusiasm the expanding nation, has been changed for golden streets and heaven's royal welcome. But, turning away from the ashes of the heroes of the past, we hear the trumpet-blast of the incoming century demanding a new generation of heroes as valiant as those that honored the one now closed. We shall best prove our appreciation of the work of the fathers of the Church by pushing forward to greater success the work they have committed to our hands.

In an age of skepticism we must have a ministry and people standing in the first ranks of learning and intelligence. With the Bible in one hand and the products of a sanctified press in the other, with the old-time fire of enthusiasm in the heart, the world will be brought to the feet of its Creator and King.

"The recollection of the honored dead should inspire us to complete what they so nobly began. That will be a degenerate age when we must go to the cemetery to find our greatest men. The lives of the fathers are not presented to us to dwarf our stature by contrast, but to show to what giants we should grow with better opportunities.

"The dead but opened the door through which the living may pass to victory. If we ourselves would prove worthy of our ancestry we shall haste forward with their memories to speed us on, so that when we have borne our age yet nearer paradise our children may strew vio'ets on our sepulchers and evoke from us, as all from our fathers, the inspiration of the immortal dead." The opening century beckons us onward and upward until our work is crowned immortal and victorious.

One hundred years from this new generations will gather together as we do to-night, to celebrate the achievements of the second century in the history of the Book Concern. The records, instead of coming from New York and Cincinnati alone, will come from China, Japan, India, Europe, and Africa, in each of which will have arisen establishments, far surpassing our own, which shall send forth their streams of light and knowledge for the elevation and salvation of our race.

When that grand celebration shall come, though we may not mingle with the throng, I am sure our King of heaven will allow us to gather on some mountain height and look down with rapture upon the scene, and heaven will be the sweeter when sower and reaper shall rejoice together.

Dr. Leonard followed, his topic being "The Missionary Society."

Address of Rev. A. B. Leonard, D.D.

Mr. Chairman and Christian Friends, The Missionary Society, which was organized April 5, 1819, and which celebrates to-night its seventieth anniversary, measures as does no other organization the growth, benevolence, courage, and conquering power of the Methodist Episcopal Church. The founders of this Society, among whom were ministers and laymen, deserve the honorable place they now occupy on the roll of Methodist history. The first officers of the Society were Bishop William McKendree, President; Bishop Enoch George, First Vice-President; Bishop Robert R. Roberts, Second Vice-President; Rev. Nathan Bangs, Third Vice-President; Mr. Francis Hall, Clerk; Mr. Daniel Ayres, Recording Secretary; Rev. Thomas Mason, Corresponding Secretary, and Rev. Joshua Soule, Treasurer. ﹅

The Corresponding Secretaries who have served this Society, exclusive of those now in office, are Thomas Mason, Nathan Bangs, William Capers, E. R. Ames, Charles Pitman, John P. Durbin, R. L. Dashiell, T. M. Eddy, J. M. Reid, and Charles H. Fowler. In 1860 William L. Harris was elected Assistant Corresponding Secretary, and in 1864 J. M. Trimble was elected to the same office. All these have gone to their reward except J. M. Reid, the historian of Methodist missions, Charles H. Fowler, an honored Bishop of the Church, and J. M. Trimble, a member of every General Conference since 1844.

This Society, like many other things connected with Methodism, was a development or an evolution necessitated by the inherent forces of the organization from which it sprang. From the first Methodism was an evangelistic force, or, if you please, a Missionary movement. This was the secret of its marvelous growth in the early years of her history. As the denomination enlarged it was found that the entire body could not be wielded in a satisfactory manner for aggressive movements in destitute regions at home and in foreign fields, and a m re compact organization, that would concentrate and render available the resources of the entire system, was the need of the hour. The circumstances which seemed to have given direction to the forces that produced the Missionary Society were peculiar, and illustrate the saying of the sometimes melancholy Cowper:

> "God moves in a mysterious way
> His wonders to perform."

The conversion of John Stewart, a poor, intemperate colored man at Marietta, Ohio, in 1816, was followed by a journey through a trackless forest, in obedience to what he believed to be the call of God, to Upper Sandusky, and the opening of a mission among the Wyandot Indians. The revival that prevailed among these Indians sent a thrill of missionary fervor through the whole Church, and led to the organization of the Missionary Society three years later. This Society from that time to the present has had much to do with the rapid movements of the Methodist itinerancy, growth of the Church, and the founding of kindred benevolent institutions.

Eight years after the organization of the Missionary Society, and inspired by it, came the Sunday School Union and Tract Societies. These societies represented a new form of missionary activity which has grown to wonderful proportions. The Sunday-School Union and Tract Societies have been, and now are, mighty missionary forces in the South, on the Western frontier, and in foreign lands.

The Church now moved on until in 1864, when another benevolent form of work was organized, known as the Church Extension Society. This Society came at the opportune period in our national history. The war was drawing to a close, and soon the whole South, which had been closed against us since 1844, was to be thrown open. Out of the Old South the New South was to be evolved. The millions of colored people made free by the exigencies of the war were to be lifted up to a useful citizenship, and the sentiments of the white population toward both freedmen and the conquering North were to undergo an important transformation. In the accomplishment of this task the Methodist Episcopal Church was to take an important part. Then, with the close of the war, there was to be an unparalleled migration westward from the Eastern States. Railroad trains were to take the place of horse, ox, and mule trains, and the people were to go in hundreds where they had gone in tens before. During the closing period of the war money accumulated in the treasury of the Missionary Society amounting to almost a half-million dollars. The treasury was burdened with the *surplus*, you see, and the authorities were troubled as to the disposition to be made of it. When the war was over the authorities of the Missionary Society comprehended the reason for the surplus of funds in its hands. It now had the means with which to send itinerants into the South and to the frontier more numerously than ever before, and the golden opportunity was not allowed to go unimproved. The funds of the Missionary treasury were just what was needed to oil the wheels of the itinerancy. These two agencies have given Methodism its supremacy in the South and West.

As to our occupancy of the South, that is a settled question. We are there, and the recent outrages committed against some of our missionaries will not cause us to call a retreat. The Joiner outrage, so recently committed, only increases our determination to remain in the South and continue to preach a gospel of equality for all men. The cruelties inflicted upon the colored people of the South must cease; they are citizens; they are there to stay; no scheme of Southern white men for their deportation to a foreign land will succeed. Their deportation is a physical impossibility. If the whole fleet of ships now sailing under the United States flag were to be employed solely for their deportation they could not carry away even the annual increase. Besides, they are needed in the South. But for their presence vast regions would be without inhabitants and without laborers, and the result would be the return of the wolf, the bear, and the buffalo. The deportation of the whites of the South would be less damaging in many localities than that of the blacks, as there would be removed a more blood-thirsty and less industrious element. The South must become as safe a place of residence for both colored and white as is the North, and the Methodist Episcopal Church must do its part in bringing about this desirable end.

To-day Methodism leads all other denominations in the great Central West and in the regions beyond. In journeying westward when you pass the line that divides Pennsylvania and Ohio you are on Methodist territory. In Ohio, Indiana, Illinois, Iowa, and Kansas, Methodism is the foremost of all denominations; indeed, it is claimed that there are more Methodists in the two States last named than of all other denominations combined. I suppose this is one reason why they have prohibition in those States. Methodists in those States live up to the standard erected by our Church in regard to the traffic in strong drink better than we do in the Eastern States.

Well, through the agency of the Missionary Society Methodist Episcopal Churches were organized rapidly in the West immediately succeeding the close of the war. But they were societies without houses of worship, and the people were not able to build. Here was a demand for a new form of missionary work, and the Church extension Society was called into existence. Since 1864 this Society has aided in erecting more than 7,000 houses of worship, while the whole Church has erected about 14,000, and still moves on, building "two a day."

Two years later another missionary agency came into existence—the Freedmen's Aid Society. Through the work accomplished in the South, largely by the Missionary Society, a multitude of people of all colors were gathered into the Methodist Episcopal Church. The South previous to the war made no provision for education at the public expense for either white or colored. Here was a field for educational effort. The colored people were the most needy, and so received the first assistance. Later our work has been enlarged, and now includes both white and colored. What was at first "the Freedmen's Aid Society" is now "the Freedmen's Aid and Southern Education Society." This Society has erected about forty institutions of learning, and during the last year gave instruction to about 8,000 students.

In 1872, seeing the need of educational facilities for young people who might desire to enter the ministry, and particularly the mission field, and who were not able to secure a thorough education at their own expense, there was organized the Board of Education—an institution that has been instrumental in sending not a few heroic spirits to recruit the ranks of our missionary army.

In 1833 the Missionary Society commenced work in the foreign field by founding a Mission in Liberia on the West coast of Africa. The foreign work has expanded until at this time we have twelve Annual Conferences and nine organized Missions. In these foreign missions there are 148 missionaries, besides other workers numbering 3,012, making a working force of 3,160, with a lay membership, including probationers, of about 65,000.

To render our work in foreign lands more effective in reaching the female populations, the Woman's Foreign Missionary Society was organized in 1869. This Society has sent out 150 missionaries, 100 of whom are now in the foreign field.

In 1881 the women of Methodism, seeing the need of work among neglected home populations in our great cities, in the South, on the frontier, and among the Indians, where the Missionary Society had opened the way, and where re-enforcements were greatly needed, organized the Woman's Home Missionary Society. Thus one after another these different forms of missionary work have come into existence, as the Missionary Society has prepared the way.

This Society measures the benevolent spirit of the Church. The ordinary forms of church work do not deserve to be classified as benevolent. It is not properly a benevolence to aid in erecting a church in which the donor expects to worship, or contribute to the current expenses of a church with which he is identified. We cannot, therefore, measure the benevolent spirit of a Church by the number of elegant houses of worship it erects or the liberality with which current expenses are supported. Nor can we measure the benevolence of a Church by the large gifts of a few wealthy men made for special purposes. Thank God for a Daniel Drew, who founds a theological seminary, and for a Jacob Sleeper, who founds a university, and for a George I. Seney, who founds a hospital! But these gifts do not measure the benevolence of the Church as a whole. The Missionary Society and the other societies, for which it has prepared the way, are the thermometer which marks the rising benevolence of the entire body, for the reason that their support comes from the multitude rather than from the few.

This Society gives expression to the courageous spirit of Methodism. This spirit is not manifested by laymen who occupy cushioned pews in elegant houses of worship or by ministers who preach to highly-cultivated and wealthy congregations. The courage of the Church is seen in those laymen and ministers who go into the haunts of wickedness in our great cities, and to the frontier to live in dug-outs, planting Christian Churches and ministering to the neglected and vicious; who go to foreign countries and hold the red-hot battle-line that divides Christianity and heathenism. Bishop Taylor journeying on foot through the jungles of Africa, sleeping on the ground with the open sky for shelter, fighting malaria, and preaching the Gospel to the naked heathen, is the type of heroism which the Church needs to bring this sin-stricken world to Christ. If all cannot heroically go to these hard and dangerous fields, all can heroically work and give and sacrifice to support such as do go.

This Society measures also the conquering power of the Church. The Church is an army of invasion and conquest. It is under orders from its great Captain to conquer the world and bring it into subjection to his sway. The Missionary Society brings every soldier into line and gives him a chance to fight for his crown. There is no form of superstition or heathenism, however deeply seated or hoary with age, that this Society needs to fear, backed, as it is, by a courageous Church. Thank God, we have no occasion to spend our time in devising a second probation, revising our creed, or establishing our claim to apostolic succession! We believe in one fair probation for all, that Jesus Christ died for all, and that all are in the only succession worth talking about who fight and *win.* Our song is:

> " Sure I must fight, if I would reign,
>   Increase my courage, Lord;
> I'll bear the toil, endure the pain,
>   Supported by thy word.
>
> " Thy saints in all this glorious war
>   Shall conquer, though they die;
> They see the triumph from afar,
>   By faith they bring it nigh."

General Clinton B. Fisk spoke on "The Founders of the Methodist Book Concern" as follows:

General Fisk's Address.

Bishop Andrews, Dear Fathers, and Brethren, "What mean ye by this service?" Moses, the great deliverer, prophet, and leader, in his last discourse unto all the congregation of Israel prior to their hasty departure out of the land of Egypt, and on the eve of that dreadful night when the shadow of death fell across the threshold of every Egyptian abode and the destroying angel passed over the homes of the children of Israel, bade them observe this thing for an ordinance to them and their sons forever; that when their children should in the after generations say unto them "What mean ye by this service?" then the story of the sacrifice and the redemption should be told them. Running along the centuries we hear the Psalmist's outburst of song, "The sayings which we have heard and known, and our fathers have told us, we will not hide them from their children, showing to the generation to come the praises of the Lord, and his strength and his wonderful works that he hath done."

If our children make the inquiry of us to-night, "What mean ye by this service?" our answer will be: "That the sayings which we have heard and known respecting the genesis of the Methodist Book Concern we will not hide them from our children, but will show to the generations to come the wonderful work of the Lord through the publishing and missionary enterprises of the Methodist Episcopal Church."

Our theme for brief utterance is "The Founders of the Methodist Book Concern." The founders—who were they? First of all was its foundress: that remarkable woman, the matron of Epworth Rectory, the mother of John and Charles

Wesley, who in the early years of the eighteenth century, while rocking the cradle in which slept the annual contribution to the family circle, reached her hand across the gulf of half a century and rocked the cradle of Methodism. In all galleries of noble and illustrious men and women Susannah Wesley deserves a foremost place. She was exemplary in the discharge of every social and parental duty. The completeness of her character shone forth in all the sweet sanctities of her home. The night would be far spent before we could speak of a tithe of the excellencies of that queenly, sagacious, common-sense mother, and pattern of all womanly virtues. The mother of the Wesleys impressed her sons John and Charles with the value of good books, good study, and good use of printer's ink. Her daily, and specially Thursday, hours with her darling "Jacky," as she was wont to call John Wesley, were the beginnings of Wesley's Book Concern.

At thirty years of age Mr. Wesley had written his first volume, and he kept on writing until hundreds of volumes in prose written by himself, and the Christian lyrics, which fairly streamed from the inspired pen of Charles Wesley, crowded the shelves of English libraries. Wesley's first publication was that of a book of devotions, issued at a very low price, for the poor. His edition of the *Imitation of Christ* followed, and from that time forward his busy pen at home and on his long and swift journeys as an itinerant on his national circuit and every-where, and his busy types at the Old Foundry, scattered cheap tracts and books by the ten thousand, as instrumentalities for spreading religious knowledge through Great Britain and among the Methodist societies springing up on this continent.

At the first Conference held in this country, that of 1773, in the city of Philadelphia, the publication and sale of Mr. Wesley's books by proper authority received careful consideration and Conference direction.

The pioneer of the Methodist Book Concern on American soil was Robert Williams; a fiery, earnest expounder of the faith of the Wesleys. In 1769, learning of the progress of Methodism in the New World, Robert Williams sought permission of John Wesley to leave England and preach the Gospel in America. He received authority to emigrate to this country and preach if he would subordinate himself to the missionaries Boardman and Pillmoor. The young circuit-rider sold his horse to pay his English debts and hastened to the nearest seaport, carrying his saddle-bags on his arm, and set off for the ship with a loaf of bread and a bottle of milk, but not a penny of money for his passage. Ashton, an ardent young Irish friend, paid his fare to New York, where he landed in advance of the missionaries, and immediately began to preach in John Street. Robert Williams was a slight, agile, restless little man. His friends wondered that so large a soul could find room in so small a body. His rich voice rolled like music upon his charmed listeners, as if he were a harper playing upon all harps at his pleasure. He first printed books for American Methodists. He established the first Methodist circuit in Virginia. He was the first Methodist minister that married, the first that located, the first that died in this country. His beautiful, active life and work for six years in spreading scriptural holiness in this new land was an epic. He it was in the hand of God who brought from darkness to light Jesse Lee. What honor to the spiritual father of that heroic itinerant, the founder of Methodism in New England! Francis Asbury laid Robert Williams to rest, and by his now unknown grave in Virginia said that probably no man in America had been equally successful in awakening souls.

At repeated Conferences after the death of Robert Williams the necessity for a Book Concern established by the Church was discussed. At the Christmas Conference in 1784, among the rules of ministerial life we find, sandwiched between that protesting against late suppers and wine-drinking and an exhortation to go on to perfection, this injunction : " Be active in dispersing Mr. Wesley's books. Every assistant may beg money of the rich to buy books for the poor." Not until 1789, at a Conference held in New York, was definite action taken, and a Book Agent—or Book Steward, as he was then termed— appointed.

One hundred years ago last May there convened twenty men in a Methodist Conference in the old preaching-house in John Street, New York. Let us look in upon them as they enter upon their great work by singing :

> " And are we yet alive
> And see each other's face ?
> .   .   .   .
> " What troubles have we seen,
>   What conflicts have we passed,
> Fightings without and fears within,
>   Since we assembled last !
> But out of all the Lord
>   Hath brought us by his love,
> And still he does his help afford,
>   And hides our life above."

Chiefest among that score of God's chosen ministers of reconciliation and peace sat Francis Asbury, pioneer Bishop of the Methodist Episcopal Church, then forty-four years of age, in the beginning of his prime, in the broad daylight of one of the most useful lives ever known among men. He had been laying broad and deep the foundations of the Methodist Episcopal Church in the valleys and on the mountains of the Atlantic coast. He had been flying, like the apocalyptic angel having the everlasting Gospel to preach, over all the settled regions

5

from New York to North Carolina. With what emphasis he
declared to that handful of believers in John Street: "The
Lord is my witness, that if my whole body, yea, every hair of
my head, could labor and suffer, they should freely be given
up for God and souls." He who, when the wicked mob pur-
sued him, had mounted his trusty horse, and, as he rode on
through forest and swamp and peril, made the woods ring
with the song :

> "The rougher the way, the shorter our stay ;
> The tempests that rise
> Shall gloriously hurry our souls to the skies."

A mighty man was Francis Asbury! By his side sat one of
his juniors in years, the strong-souled, scholarly, consecrated
missionary, Bishop Thomas Coke. He who, as the foreign
minister of Methodism, had been commissioned by John
Wesley—who was led to do so by a wisdom not his own—to
visit America and to assist in the organization of our Methodism as a Church distinct and separate from the Church of our
fathers over the sea. Sitting in that goodly company was
Richard Whatcoat, the humble, holy, and self-devoted man,
a member of the Coke embassy from England to the infant
Church in America, and who had once been a fellow class-leader
with Asbury at Wednesbury. And there, too, was Jesse Lee,
thirty-one years of age ; that man of deep spirituality, yet of
" infinite jest and most excellent fancy," whose rare rich humor,
blended with his fearless, honest dignity, and all-abounding
grace, made him an easy victor in every field of conflict, whether
it was with the warm-hearted Virginians or the cool, intellectual New Englanders. God give to our modern Methodism
a legion of Jesse Lees, men of firm but gentle natures, which,
like sunbeams, shine without an effort and leave us genial, like

themselves! By the side of Jesse Lee in the Conference of 1789 sat John, his brother; dignified, zealous and untiring in his calling as a Methodist preacher. Not far away from the platform sat one in the thirty-seventh year of his life, in the very syllables of whose name there was music; a man strong and tender, distressingly self-diffident, yet full of fiery heroism, whose labors, abundant for more than half a century, are a complete record of our contemporaneous church history. Freeborn Garrettson's name was and is a household word throughout this land. Near by sat one who had been among the bravest soldiers in the army of the Revolution. He had been a special favorite of Washington. He had abandoned his college life to draw a sword for liberty. He had fallen seriously wounded in leading the advance up the heights of Flatbush at the battle of Long Island. He had become a soldier of the cross, a standard-bearer in the army of the Lord, a faithful Methodist preacher, the builder of and the first to preach in our Forsyth Street Church—that man of blessed memory, Thomas Morrell.

At the table of the secretary sat one whose name and fame will go ringing down the ages so long as the history of the Methodist Book Concern shall be read. He had been the honor man in his class at Eton College, and from his entrance upon his work as a Methodist preacher in this country had stood in the front rank of that brave and brotherly host. He was among those who sat in the Christmas Conference, where he was a leader in every debate. He made the motion that gave to our Church the name of Methodist Episcopal. Asbury said of him: " He is a man of great piety, great skill in learning, drinks in Greek and Latin swiftly, yet prays much, and walks close with God." The Minutes said of him when he died: " He was one of the greatest characters that ever graced the pulpit or adorned the society of the Methodists." Such was John Dickins, then at the age of forty-three. "Time would fail me to tell" of Phœbus and Cloud, of Durham and Willis and McClaskey and others of that memorable Conference of one hundred years ago.

O rare and sacred fellowship! Like the disciples in the Jerusalem chamber, they were of one accord. They were the immediate founders of the Methodist Book Concern. Three great events distinguished the proceedings of that Conference.

1. It was the first religious body to extend congratulations to George Washington, who had then just been inaugurated the first President of the United States.

2. It commissioned Jesse Lee as the apostle of Methodism to New England.

3. It established the Methodist Book Concern. Thomas Coke, in writing of that remarkable Conference, said : " It was all peace and concord. Glory! glory be to God! We have now settled our printing business." It was an easy thing to resolve unanimously, as they did, that the Book Concern of the Methodist Episcopal Church should be established on a secure basis and on a large scale ; that the profits of the books should be applied "partly to finish and pay off the debt on Cokesbury College and partly to establish missions and schools among the Indians ; " but where was the capital to come from with which to initiate the great undertaking?

The Conference, as a committee of the whole, were almost in despair as they considered the deep poverty of themselves and the societies scattered through the country. Up rose John Dickins and said: " Brethren, be of good courage and go forward ; I have one hundred and twenty pounds sterling ($600), the savings from my life's labors. I will lend every shilling of it to the Methodist Book Concern until such time as it can be returned to me." The Conference joyfully and gratefully accepted the loan, and by unanimous vote elected John Dickins as Book Steward. On August 17, 1789, at No. 43 Fourth Street, Philadelphia, John Dickins with his own hand made entry of the first transactions of the Methodist Book Concern. The first book issued was Wesley's abridged translation of Thomas à Kempis's immortal *Imitation of Christ*—a good corner-stone on which to build the ever-increasing business and world-wide influence of our publishing house whose centenary we this night celebrate. John Dickins, by the blessing of God upon his pioneer labors, started a series of influences whose vibrations reach to the uttermost parts of the earth and to the latest time. All honor to the heroic founders of the Methodist Book Concern! By the memories of their lives and deeds, by all the impulse and inspiration of the present hour, by the noblest instincts of our own souls, in the spirit of rejoicing consecration let us, who are honored to be their sons and daughters, be faithful to our magnificent inheritance, and to Him whose sovereign spirit touches our souls and makes our hearts glad as we stand upon the threshold of a new century, with its grander work, with its nobler heroism, and its assured conquests; and may our great conquering Church, in all its revolving cycles of history, in its every agency, increasingly have for its inspiration that blessed assurance which gave the dying Wesley such consolation when the everlasting sunrise burst in upon failing heart and flesh, " The best of all is, God is with us."

J. M. Buckley, D.D., LL.D., was the last speaker. His subject was "Methodist Literature."

Dr. Buckley's Address.

When Methodism arose it needed a literature for explanation, for defense, for propagation, and for instruction. For explanation, because it was misunderstood; for defense, because it was assaulted and traduced; for propagation, because its ministers were itinerant and the supply inadequate to the need; for instruction, because its converts were generally uneducated, especially in the principles of religion. Nor did the need diminish as the denomination grew in numbers, activity, and social position. An illustration from a later period may suffice. At first it affiliated with the American Tract Society and the American Sunday-School Union; but their publications were exclusively Calvinistic, and became germs of doctrinal discord. This gave rise to the formation of our own Tract Society and Sunday-School Union. The more discussion, the more inquiry; hence the demand for publications to remove misunderstandings, satisfy curiosity, and unify opinion.

The system of government and administration is complex, its appointments for transient periods, its Conferences of frequent occurrence. Times and seasons depending upon personal arrangement are liable to frequent revision and change, the usages of the denomination numerous and peculiar, all of which required communications constant, full, and authoritative to both pastors and people. Besides, the type of religious experience being devotional and emotional to an unusual degree demanded for its perpetuation and cultivation an unusual amount of easily-assimilated religious reading, of all things the most difficult to produce and consequently to procure. Methodism was compelled to create from its indigenous resources the greater part of its essential nutriment for the spiritual life, and to edit what it reprinted from other denominations. Such supplies were all the more important because of the great use made of local preachers, the ignorance of many of the traveling preachers, and the necessity of class-leaders, all of whom were required to give instruction in spiritual things.

Another function subserved by Methodist literature was to

develop a class of competent writers and to afford them a market for their literary products. This was of much greater importance in the beginning than it is now; for Methodists, except in the case of men of transcendent intellect and conspicuous position, were ostracized, or, at best, satirized. Also printing and publication establishments were comparatively few, and access to the people was correspondingly difficult. To-day Methodist writers of ability can reach the best minds in the denomination and the public at large through magazines, books, and the press generally. Nor when they write upon general subjects do they suffer in the popular estimate materially because of their denominational views; gaining sometimes as much consideration from publishers and editors because of the great constituency supposed to be interested in them as they lose in some directions because of the monopoly of literary culture which certain circles still affect, it being, however, rather a reminiscence than an actual possession.

Methodist literature, therefore, naturally classifies itself. Its most conspicuous function is to furnish regular denominational supplies; and, if we construct the pyramid philosophically, at the base are the *doctrinal* works. It has published and kept continually on hand the works of John Wesley; the American edition consisting of seven volumes, two of which comprise the sermons, and the rest miscellanies; these miscellaneous works are paralleled in interest only by Boswell's *Life of Johnson*, between which there is vastly more similarity than any who have not critically read both would imagine. Watson's *Institutes* and sermons, the former, subject to proper deduction for the errors of his time, illustrating in a high degree Emerson's idea of good writing, which is, "to see clearly and state lucidly." Fletcher's *Checks* and *Miscellaneous Writings*, useful to a past generation of Methodists, are by no means obsolete yet; and Pope's great, though peculiar, work upon *Theology.*

Of *commentaries* it has produced a host. Benson, once widely used. Adam Clarke, unabridged, in six sturdy volumes; abridged, and with a new personality introduced by Daniel Curry. Whedon's Commentary, containing as its presiding genius the best thought of the acute and vigorous intellect of its editor; the painstaking work of a Hunter; the last great work of a Newhall; the scholarly annotations of Professor Terry; besides excellent work by Drs. Daniel Steele, J. K. Burr, A. B. Hyde, Henry Bannister, F. D. Hemenway, and F. G. Hibbard. Nor must I forget the work to which thousands of ministers and laymen in the prime of life owe so much for instruction received in the formative period, Longking's *Notes on the Gospels,* which had a definiteness and grasp not always found in more modern publications.

Speaking generally, we may say that the Book Concern has published a large majority of the works included in the Conference Studies ordered by the Bishops, under the instruction of the General Conference, to be used by the local and traveling ministers in preparation for the examinations on which their promotion and ordination depend. Akin to these works are the great *histories* by which it is possible for succeeding generations to say reverently, "We have heard with our ears, O Lord; our fathers have told us what works thou didst in their days, in the times of old." Of these, that of Nathan Bangs is forcible because he was so great a part of what he describes; while the more elaborate, artistic, and jubilant volumes of Abel Stevens remain as a priceless possession, having the power of instruction, and at the same time stimulating to a holy imitation and emulation the hearts of those who read them. Besides these there are many local histories and abridge-

ments which have done for the denomination what similar
works do for the country.

In the domain of *biography* the productions of Methodism
have been numerous, and the sales immense in the aggregate.
Nor is it possible to overestimate the beneficent influence of
properly written religious biographies. Of course, discrimi-
nating persons know that absolutely truthful biographies are
not written, because of the limitations of human nature as to
knowledge, space, and the effects of personal bias. But they
perpetuate ideals and furnish inspiring models; and in religious biographies, if the type of excellence sometimes discour-
ages, it may tend to the natural working out of what is
possible to the reader, even though he loses all hope of becoming exactly what he admires in the portraiture before him.
When the biography is that of a person with whom we have
been contemporaneous, its intellectual effect is not to be
despised, for the mind continually compares its own impres-
sions with the lineaments depicted upon the page.

Meanwhile stupendous masses of *Sabbath-school* literature of
the most varying degrees of ability, from the highest to such
as on another occasion it would be proper to criticise adversely,
have been poured forth, teaching the young idea how to shoot,
sometimes at a mark, sometimes without a mark, but upon the
whole much better adapted to the purpose than would result
from promiscuous selections.

The periodical literature of the Church deserves separate
treatment. The *Methodist Magazine* is not known to the
present generation, and, when taken from the shelves where it
has reposed by the grandchildren of those who read it, its con-
tents seem singularly dry, and remote from the spirit of this
age. This impression, however, passes away when the time
that it appeared and its purpose are taken into the account. It

gave place to the *Quarterly Review*, which, after various mutations, under the universally accomplished McClintock, the
subtle, tenacious, witty, and versatile Whedon, and the intellectually athletic yet agile Curry, is at the present time, as a
bimonthly, under the editorship of Dr. Mendenhall, enjoying a
larger circulation than it ever had, and, being in the midst of
an unfinished polemical conflict upon recondite principles of
criticism, is attracting more attention than has been given to it
for many years. The *Ladies' Repository*, begun before the
great development of magazine literature, for a number of
years filled an important place ; but restricted in competition
with outside enterprise, and modified by the changed relation
of women to society and to public discussion, gradually declined. Prior to this period the attempt had been made to
publish a general magazine, under the name of the *National
Magazine*. As might have been foreseen, this periodical
failed, not for want of ability in its editor, nor, speaking
generally, in its contributors, but for want of adaptability.
The demand for it, as it was, was not sufficient, and it was not
available as a supply for a different demand. The transforming of the *Ladies' Repository* into the *National Repository*
was another attempt of a denominational publishing house to
furnish a popular magazine regardless of past experiences,
handicapped with fatal defects and incompetences, in competition with the most extraordinary development of modern
times, sustained by lavish outlays, catering to every taste, and
managed with consummate ability, paid for on a scale that
would be destructive to the necessary simplicity of a religious
management.

The *weekly periodicals* of the Church are in their circulation
the admiration of the religious world, and as they are so frequently seen must be left to speak for themselves. It is suffi-

cient to affirm that without them it would be impossible to carry forward the work of the Church efficiently, and if left exclusively to undenominational or private supplies a plentiful sowing of dragon's teeth would be likely. The existence of unofficial and undenominational publications, and the freedom of speech exercised, and consequent diversity of opinions held by the management of the official press upon all subjects except the fundamentals of Methodism, make it certain that every thing that should be will be heard.

The *limitations* of a denominational literature are that the general public will invariably consider the institution a part of Methodist machinery, and infer, therefore, that what it publishes is primarily for the use of Methodists, and its imprint will constantly confirm that impression. So that, from a commercial point of view, what is its chief strength is of necessity an element of restriction. Of course, all works of fiction of a purely sentimental character, especially those that are sensational, and whose sales run up into the hundreds of thousands, are excluded from the list; and the notoriety, not to say fame, which the house would obtain by their publication, and which is of immense business value to many other houses, is not within the reach of the Book Concern. No intelligent person, however, regards what is essential to the accomplishment of the end he has in view in the light of an undesirable limitation.

Naturally the demands of its customers would lead it to a considerable extent into the general book trade; and it has published, in the aggregate, an immense number of works of travel, harmless fiction, general biography, history, science, and has done a large amount of business of which the Chautauqua publications may serve as an illustration. The number of works in its General Catalogue is several thousand, many

of which are of the highest grade intellectually. The travels
of Dr. Durbin and the works of Stephen Olin in their time at-
tracted great attention, as did Thomson's *Essays: Educational, Moral, and Religious*, and his *Evidences of Religion*.
Whedon *On the Will*, by the comparatively few who were
competent to comprehend it, and patient enough to read it, has
been placed upon the shelf by the side of that most potential
work, *On the Will*, by Jonathan Edwards, as representing a
battle of two schools and two intellectual giants.

Among the more recent works which have attained a high
place are Hurst's *History of Rationalism*, and *Bibliotheca
Theologica*, notably Harmon's *Introduction to the Study of
the Scriptures*, Terry's *Hermeneutics*, and Professor Bennett's
great work on *Christian Archæology*. Professor Bowne first
commanded attention by his *Philosophy of Herbert Spencer*
and *Studies in Theism*. Mrs. Amelia E. Barr, continually
increasing in reputation as a writer in pure fiction, reached a
large constituency of readers through three of her stories published by this house. Many other entertaining and elevating
romances for the young have been brought out, of which
A Damsel of the Nineteenth Century, by Miss Norris is a type
of the best. Nor should the great work of Dr. Dorchester,
*Christianity in the United States from the First Settlement
Down to the Present Time*, and that smaller but very important publication by the same author, *The Problem of Religious
Progress*, be omitted. The house is at the present time en-
gaged in publishing the life work of Bishop Foster in a series of
volumes upon Theology, which, if completed according to the
plan, will constitute a library in themselves. Not in the whole
course of its history has it published works of a higher grade
intellectually and critically than within the past few years.

Ready to adapt itself to modern methods, it established a

Subscription-Book Department, through which an immense number of most useful books have been sold. *The People's Cyclopedia*, which is being constantly revised, and has received the highest commendation and very little adverse criticism, of which so far as true its editors availed themselves at once, correcting the errors and supplying the defects pointed out, has already reached the enormous sale of one hundred and two thousand copies, which at the ordinary retail price would amount to $1,550,000.

Since the purchase of the plates of Ridpath's *History of the United States* one hundred and fifty thousand copies have been sold, while his *History of the World*, more recently published, has reached a sale of sixty-five thousand, which, in the absence of more elaborate works, is useful to the people. Dr. Dorchester's book on the *Liquor Problem* has had a wide sale through the same department, and at the present time the *People's Cyclopedia*, *History of the World*, and of the *United States*, each average a sale of nearly one thousand copies per month.

For a hundred years Methodism has kept its presses at work. You have already heard from the senior Agent something of the extent of the business. In all these years nothing irreligious has been printed; nothing immoral; every thing adapted to promote the interests of the country and of the individual citizen. Successive generations of Methodist writers have been raised up under the influence of the spirit of Methodist literature. Many of them are still in the denomination; and men of brilliant qualities and attainments, who fill important spheres connected with other denominations, or of a purely literary character, are sons and grandsons of those who were educated chiefly through the influence of Methodist literature, without which, and the moral effects of its religious services, they might have been in ignorance and obscurity.

It is this literature which fills seminaries and colleges with students. Without it those who direct the education of the young would either have no interest in intellectual culture, or divert those whom they influenced to other sources of instruction.

But perhaps the greatest work accomplished by Methodist literature has been to counteract the natural tendencies of strong religious emotion to fanaticism. Without it the holy fervor inspired by the first preachers would have run into excesses pernicious to the mind and heart and the body, and instead of being to-day coherent, progressive, and stable, Methodism would be dead or dying.

www.ingramcontent.com/pod-product-compliance
Lightning Source LLC
Chambersburg PA
CBHW020230090426
42735CB00010B/1631